Listening to Your Soul

Listening to Your Soul

A spiritual direction workbook

Julia Mourant

CANTERBURY
PRESS
Norwich

© Julia Mourant 2022

First published in 2022 by the Canterbury Press Norwich

Editorial office
3rd Floor, Invicta House
108–114 Golden Lane
London EC1Y OTG, UK
www.canterburypress.co.uk

Canterbury Press is an imprint of Hymns Ancient & Modern Ltd
(a registered charity)

Hymns Ancient & Modern® is a registered trademark of
Hymns Ancient & Modern Ltd
13A Hellesdon Park Road, Norwich,
Norfolk NR6 5DR, UK

British Library Cataloguing in Publication data
A catalogue record for this book is available
from the British Library

ISBN 978 1-78622-336-4

Typeset by Regent Typesetting
Printed and bound in Great Britain by
CPI Group (UK) Ltd

Contents

Introduction

Soul

The language of the soul does not always find a place in everyday life, yet for anyone at all thoughtful or reflective, anyone who ponders the meaning of things, soul questions are never far away. Soul questions emerge when we wonder what the future holds for ourselves, our dear ones, our world, our planet. Soul is about connection. When you step outside your narrowly-bounded world and attend to a broader horizon, you are engaging with soul wisdom. There might be a conversation in the middle of the day, a piece of music, an unexpected gift, a surprising observation, a photograph or a memory, an awareness of joy, uncertainty or sadness, something in the news that takes us deeper into an emotional response. All these things, and countless other fleeting glimpses of something outside and beyond our tendency to tunnel vision, invite us to attend to the life of our soul.

If you could be your own best friend, that would be your soul. The soul cannot betray you: she holds wisdom, insight and experience. Where does the soul come from and what exactly is soul? Life, Belonging, Love, Being, Creativity, God, these are the vocabulary and geography of the soul. Where you find connection, creativity and becoming, you will find soul. You do not have to be religious to know that you have a soul, but it is part of the spiritual dimension of life. What is meant by 'spiritual' will depend on your perspective on life and your reference points. The word 'God' might be part of your everyday vocabulary, or not. You do not need to believe in God to read this book, or to be able to listen to your soul. Your soul will never let you down, but you have to give her a chance to speak. You can ignore soul even when she whispers, sings, or even cries to you through your body, your dreams, your thoughts, your imagination, and the events of your life. The more you listen to your soul, the more you come to trust soul wisdom. You learn from experience that when you ignore soul, you understand later what you needed to attend to. But soul never gives up, soul simply finds another way, starting from where you are.

Everyone has a soul, but the soul may be damaged, buried and perhaps asleep to the point of near death. Can a breathing human being lose their soul entirely? Possibly this is so, but it depends on whether you believe as a matter of principle that there is always hope for a soul regardless of their atrocities. I do not mean eternal salvation or 'heaven', I simply mean whether it is possible in life for a person who appears soulless to come to life and discover empathy and compassion. As the soul is invisible, we cannot know. We can only see the way people live, the way they connect. When someone stops connecting, the soul begins to wither.

You may notice that I speak of the soul as 'she'. This is traditional language which emphasizes the personal, relational nature of the soul, because a soul is not an 'it'. Think about how you relate to and name your soul. The soul is your very own soul and may have a name, or may be a she, a he, or a they. No one can tell you what to call your soul and if you listen to your soul, she will tell you. Words are rarely perfect, language is a limited tool to speak of what is beyond all vocabulary. How will you name and befriend your soul? If you desire to connect with the spiritual dimensions of life, you need to listen to her. It is possible to go through life and never look beyond the surface of things, but the beginning of spirituality is the realization that I am not the centre, nor am I at the centre, wherever that may be found. Beyond and around and beneath and above me is 'more'. What you call the 'more' depends on what you have been taught, what you have come to believe as true and trustworthy. You may know the 'more' as 'God', or you may not find religious language necessary at all.

Your soul knows the 'more' and spends time there, maybe when you are not even looking. She brings back wisdom, insight, compassion and courage and offers them to you. Your soul is that dimension of your being that connects with the Source of life, creation, being, eternity and infinity. Are you listening, are you ready? Are you longing to know what your soul wants to tell you? Do you trust that her home is with God, with deep Life, with Being?

'Soul' is one of those words we use without perhaps a clear idea of what we actually mean: it is fluid, suggestive, vague. It could mean a number of different things and possibly several things at the same time. It is hard to pin down, but a useful word when we are reaching for something that is about more than matter, more than mind. We know soul is 'spiritual' in some way, though not necessarily religious. It can apply to personality, music or food as much as to prayer.

There is something timeless about soul. Some people believe it is the element of us that lives for ever, is eternal or immortal. However, the idea of immortality is held by people in different ways. For some, it may mean eternal life with God, with some continuation of personal identity, in a realm where we reconnect with loved ones. That might be heaven, in glorious union with the saints in a place where we see God face to face, or perhaps some other home where souls and spirits live on. Alternatively, when some people speak of immortality they may mean living on in the gifts, memories, values and qualities we leave to the next generation. Some people have a strong sense that a parent, grandparent, lover or someone who has been a wise influence is 'with' them. Perhaps their life and love were so strong that it has left a permanent sense of presence. If pressed, would we say that the loved one was there? Perhaps, yes, some believe that loved ones are watching still, while others believe this is true only in a metaphorical sense. We live in the light of those we loved and who loved us, and in that sense they are with us and we are changed by them. We might believe that the love we gave somehow continues to be given, that it has power beyond our bodies. The ongoing power of love is hard to demonstrate but we might discern its fruits. To take a more grounded approach, we may focus on the fact that after our lives the molecules that made up our bodies do not cease to exist but become something else. We know that our matter will not be destroyed but will be re-formed. To say we are dust is true, and for some there is comfort in returning to 'stardust', becoming starlight, or being one with snowdrops or the ocean, trees or honeybees for a season. If this recycling of matter is the way the universe works, might not love also have some eternal endurance?

Some say animals have souls, especially animals that appear to demonstrate intelligence, affection or loyalty. Such qualities are hard to prove since it is all too easy to project human motivations and intentions onto pets. Although it is clear that there is real relationship with some creatures, while less so with ants, wasps or worms, it would be very hard to construct a convincing argument for which creatures have souls or not. You could argue that all life is ensouled, and then you have to consider what does and does not have life. In one sense a rock has life, even though it does not move or procreate. But a rock is of the living earth, and in its cracks and crevices organisms find a place to thrive and grow. We might wonder how a rock began its existence: some are formed from creatures and trees that have been fossilized. This process would have involved energy, and where there is energy there is surely life.

No one can isolate a soul – it will forever be something we hold sacred but cannot capture. The Celtic saints sometimes spoke of seeing a soul ascend from the body of a holy person at the point of death. When we read these tales, we may wonder how literally to take them, and whether what was seen had some material, observable nature, or whether it was spiritually perceived.

There is wisdom in saying we do not know, but what we cannot do is dismiss the idea of soul altogether, unless you believe that human beings are simply animals who are born to live and die, and there is no context beyond the arbitrariness of matter. But whatever your beliefs, it is hard even for an atheist to say there is no connection between living things, and once you have connection, you need a word for it which points to the realm beyond time, space and matter. Soul has proved a good word for these things, even if it is imprecise.

The idea of soul is often used outside explicitly spiritual contexts. It may refer to the depth of connection in art or music, dance, painting, sculpture, food or architecture. A building that we consider to be soulless might be a place that seems lifeless and without any power to evoke life, love or relationship. A place, or something that has been made or cooked or written without soul, will never resonate with our inner being or connect beyond being interesting or technically accomplished. Perhaps soul is the added life. My soul makes me, me and not someone else, and that cannot be destroyed. When I am gone, my soul may find a place in the hearts of those who remember me. Perhaps soul even lives on when no one at all remembers me. If you have ever visited a historic site, such as a battlefield or ancient monastery, you may have a sense of the nameless souls, ordinary people, who lived and died there. Perhaps this is sentimentality or romanticism, nevertheless it is a hard-hearted person who can stand among ancient ruins and not wonder, listen a little, dig for a moment into imagination. In such places we ask, 'Who is here now? What remains? Is some part of the past locked here, to be constantly replayed?'

If soul is essentially about connection, whether people or art or place, then it follows that soul cannot be entirely personal and individual. The language of soul comes with something of a health warning for those who think they can indulge in some kind of private soul experience of their own design. If you listen to your soul, it will tell you things that are uncomfortable. It will remind you that you are connected to others in faraway places you do not particularly want to imagine or think about. Your soul will not let you rest until you acknowledge that you cannot be isolated in your own self-referential world. Spiritual life begins with the recognition that I am not at the centre of everything, and the world is not mine to define, claim, plunder. I have no right to construct an existence that takes no account of connection. Spiritual life is essentially about connection and, once we have grasped the importance of spiritual life, we need a way of exploring connection. You can put it the other way round: once you have grasped the importance of connection, you need a way of exploring the spiritual dimension of life.

This is where we come to spiritual direction, which is the focus of this book. Spiritual direction is a place to explore connection, not a refuge for self-indulgent navel gazing. If your idea of spiritual life is about seeking disconnected experiences or supernatural phenomena, then spiritual direction will not be much help. Spiritual direction that takes no account of connection is not actually spiritual direction; it would be a conversation about me, my experience, my world, even if I wrap it in spiritual language. We will say more about spiritual direction shortly. First, having established that soul is about connection, how do we tune into that connection, listen to soul? What does it mean to listen to soul?

The starting place is to acknowledge that there is a place within us which is a well of God-given spirit wisdom, connection and insight. We will say more later about what is meant by the word 'God', but for now let's simply recognize that this soul place within us is a gift, it was given, we did not create it or make it. Some believe that this was given by God, others that it comes from Love, or perhaps Mother Earth, or Wisdom, or the Life that flows through the cosmos which we do not fully understand. Often the soul has been seen as feminine. Saint Teresa of Avila, who lived and wrote in the sixteenth century, referred to the soul as 'her'. Certainly soul is not an impersonal 'it', a force or energy without another reference point. The point of this book is not to write a philosophical consideration of the nature of soul. Simply, we know that within us there is a place of wisdom. God speaks there, it is the place of encounter, wisdom, identity, truth, connection and life.

When we speak of souls, we will soon come across the language of salvation and the variety of beliefs about what it means for souls to be saved. Interpretations and perspectives may be focused on the present or future, or both. A future expectation may envisage saved souls in heaven. However, salvation, whatever that is, can have no real meaning for our lives unless it is expressed in the here and now. We might think of the care and health at the centre of our motivation, action and compassion rather than some eternal preservation of some aspect of ourselves. We might wonder if we are saved from something or for something. My soul is saved when, free from illusion and delusion, I can take my place in the world as a human being made in the image of God and living in and from the life, compassion and grace that flows from God, or Love, or the Divine. If I have no compassion, my soul is dead. If I am unaware of my connection with all people and the earth itself, then my soul is asleep and needs saving. We have noted that soul is connection and life, but it is possible to be alive and breathing yet deeply asleep at the same time. The more we are in touch with our soul, the more we will be alive and awake rather than shut down, complacent and disengaged. Soulful music may be vibrant, joyous or mournful; soul food may be spicy or comforting, but soul is the opposite of bland, complacent, lifeless, disconnected.

With the eyes and ears of soul, the horizon is not just a view, it is the edge of the cosmos; music is not just beautiful, it is enchanting; nature is not just soothing, it is pulsing with connection and invitation and it calls to me to come on in. Soul words are words from integrity, truth and belonging. Soul words are sacred and this is why we need to listen to them. Your soul wants to tell you how to live and die. Only your soul can offer healing and renewal and hope. Your soul knows much more than you have any idea about. Your soul will not let you get away with a disconnected life. Listen, there is wisdom that will change your life.

This is a book about spiritual direction, or spiritual accompaniment as it may sometimes be called. The conversation with a spiritual director is all about listening to soul. Before we explore some themes that may emerge in spiritual direction, we will say a bit more about that conversation, where you might start and what to expect. Some people prefer to speak about a spiritual accompanier, or soul friend, or soul companion. Whatever the language, this book is about the conversation with someone who listens to you as you listen to your soul. This book mostly uses the term 'spiritual director' because that is what I am most familiar with, and it is the term I continue to use for a variety of reasons. However, I will also use the term 'spiritual accompanier', and I do not mean anything different. I will say more about this shortly.

The material in this book is intended for those exploring the idea of spiritual direction, and it may also be useful to spiritual directors who are supporting those in the early stages of learning how to use the space and in need of some starting points. If you are beginning to explore the idea of spiritual direction for yourself, perhaps you are curious but don't really know what spiritual direction is or why it might be a good thing. Perhaps someone has told you it would be just what you need, someone to talk with about the spiritual dimension of life. Or maybe you have a sense that you are looking for some place of deeper conversation that touches on meaning and eternity, but it's a bit vague. You have not quite worked out what the questions are, but you do know they are there. You don't want to be told what to think, what to believe or what to do, yet you know you can't entirely work it out on your own. You need a guide who will discuss the landmarks and wonder at them rather than march ahead and tell you to follow. A spiritual director is someone who keeps you company, listens and prompts. Some prefer the term spiritual accompanier, which particularly underlines this element of being alongside. A spiritual director will have been on their own spiritual journey, possibly travelling for quite a long time, so they are listening from the perspective of having asked a lot of hard questions without necessarily finding all the answers. In any case, they know that other people's answers are no kind of an answer at all, so they will be more interested in inviting you into an adventure and exploration on your terms than in offering any short cuts based on their individual experience. Someone else may have a great map, but if it depicts a land you are not travelling through, their map will not even be very interesting, never mind helpful. Spiritual directors know that maps are useful, but they will leave theirs on the shelf and support you as you draw in the valleys and mountain ranges, the seas and bogs and deserts and glorious vistas of your own.

If you are a spiritual director or accompanier, you will know this territory well, but there may be those who talk with you who need a few prompts as they explore their soul-world. It is quite challenging for a spiritual director or accompanier when someone comes along because they have been encouraged, or even told, by someone else that this will be a good thing. They may be genuinely willing to give it a try but not know where to start. Sometimes it is very difficult for someone who feels they have been pressed into having a conversation they were not necessarily looking for. If they are nervous or uncertain, they might seem quite passive and wait for the spiritual director to take the initiative or do most of the work. These early negotiations usually settle down as trust and understanding develop. However, no spiritual director will continue to meet with someone who really does not want to be there. Spiritual directors are not part of any system of reporting or accountability to a third party, they are completely free of external agendas. Spiritual directors never, ever, report back or discuss you with someone else. If that kind of conversation is expected then it is not spiritual direction but something else, and there will need to be clarity about the purpose of that relationship and its boundaries. It is common practice for spiritual directors never to reveal who they know and who they have conversations with. If you want to tell someone who you talk with as your spiritual accompanier, that is up to you, but the spiritual director will not tell anyone that you meet or even that they know you. Sometimes this means that if you meet in another context they may not even acknowledge you. This is not rudeness, it simply means that no one can ask what your relationship is and how you know each other. This might start a conversation requiring the kind of explanations you might both rather avoid. The role of a spiritual director is always to get out of the way.

Before we go any further, let's be clear about language. Spiritual direction and spiritual accompanying are effectively the same thing and there is no real distinction at all to be made if you are looking for someone to talk with. Some prefer one term rather than the other but that is simply because they emphasize slightly different aspects of the charism of spiritual direction. 'Charism' is a word that draws on the concept of gifting, it is another word for speaking about the vocation, gift or ministry of spiritual listening. A charism is a responsibility for a gift, often held by a group. So as the Christian tradition seeks to faithfully hold and express the charism of spiritual direction, it is done as a community. 'Spiritual direction' is traditional language which has been in use for a long time. There was a time when a spiritual director might have been perceived to be quite stern and give very definite advice and guidance, but this would be a very unusual approach now. More recently, there has been a move to speak more of 'spiritual accompaniment' because it sounds less hierarchical or authoritarian. Spiritual direction is neither hierarchical nor authoritarian and if you experience it in this way the best thing you can do is find someone else. We are much more conscious of the potential of spiritual abuse now and any accompanying relationship will only be healthy if careful boundaries are attended to in order never to coerce or dominate. In the past there was sometimes a stronger element of accountability to one's spiritual director than would be considered appropriate now. The context for spiritual direction would have been within defined faith communities with some given expectations about spiritual practice and belief. The language of accompaniment which is used today underlines the collaborative and equal nature of the relationship and is an attempt to rebalance any potential implication that the conversation might be anything less than absolutely liberating, healing and empowering. Today, spiritual directors have more training, more support and more guidance about good practice than has ever been the case, and whatever term they prefer to use they are committed to listening with confidentiality, encouragement and acceptance. You will find more information about this at the end of the book. I use the terms spiritual direction and spiritual accompaniment interchangeably because perhaps we need both terms for a fully rounded approach. Something may be lost when we abandon traditional language, but it undoubtedly needs reframing for a new context so that unhelpful overtones which may be heard in a particular way do not confuse and mislead.

This book also uses the word 'God' quite a bit. You can decide what to do with that word; people mean very different things by the God word and some would rather avoid it altogether, preferring a different vocabulary for the language of the soul. God maybe a very real presence to you, a Love you know and talk with. If you have Christian faith then you will also speak of Jesus Christ and the Holy Spirit, and you may be part of a church community. This book is for anyone on a spiritual journey and your language may be that of Source, or Spirit, or Love. When I speak of God, I mean God in the biggest sense possible – I am not limiting the idea of God to any particular religious tradition or faith context, I simply mean the Source of Life and Love and Being and Becoming and all that is. Similarly if I speak of Source, Love, Spirit or Compassion then you may prefer the word 'God'. The Christian tradition, which is the one I happen to know, largely because of the time and place of my birth, teaches that God is Love and Love is God. I make no distinction between 'God' and 'Grace' or 'Hope' and all the streams of life that come to us from that spiritual dimension which we do not own and cannot control or ever fully know or speak of. This is where the soul can dwell, and if we enter into soul conversation, the vocabulary is this language of Life and these gifts are available to us. For me, to speak of God is to speak of Grace, and to speak of Life is to speak of God. We need words, but words are like signposts or windows, which invite rather than limit. If God is the Source of all Love and Life and Grace then these things are, quite simply, God.

Soul conversation is what spiritual direction or accompaniment is all about. Listening to your soul is not always easy. There are so many voices that get in the way and confuse us. Sometimes it seems as if life is constantly shouting. Even when we are alone our lives are full of messages from electronic devices, which bring us news, gossip, advertising, entertainment and misinformation. We might be able to silence that stream of interference but there is still our inner noise. Subtle messages about our purpose, our worth, our responsibilities and our failings are always ready to induce anxiety, guilt and stress. This constant external and internal bombardment leads to sensory, emotional and spiritual overload. Our sense of who God is, who I am, what I am here for, what is important, so often gets mixed up. This is why spiritual direction or accompaniment can be such a liberating space. You are with someone who is skilled in holding a space in which the noise drops away and you can hear yourself, your soul, God, with fresh and often surprising clarity. Clarity does not arrive to order, but your accompanier is comfortable sitting with you in confusion, silence, not knowing. Being allowed to think aloud, in the presence of someone who won't judge you or tell you what to do but just believe you, is a way of slowing down and getting out of the immediate panic. Thinking aloud can include speaking the truths about how you are, what you feel, what you think, what your experience has been, without having to dress it up or pretend. It may not be the last word, and probably won't be, but to tell your own truth in the presence of God is a healing thing and sometimes we are stuck until we can do that.

Spiritual direction is about the truth of joy, wonder, sorrow and bewilderment – all the things we experience. It is not just about difficulties or problems though these may be real enough. To speak of something that has warmed your soul and brought delight allows you to look at it from more angles, appreciate it deeply, and thereby allow it to change you from within.

Spiritual direction is about allowing your soul to teach you, transform you, with the life that comes from God, the Source. It is hard to engage in that process on your own, but an attentive companion will listen, prompt, remind, invite. The spiritual accompanier is a kind of witness, who notices, who hears, who has a little distance. Your story is not their story, so they are free to notice particular words, make connections and listen to what is not said. They can offer these back as observations and wonderings, it is like holding up a mirror for you. Sometimes we need help to hear ourselves and see ourselves, and then we realize what our soul has been telling us all along.

There is a key question at the heart of spiritual direction, a question that really defines spiritual accompaniment and sets it apart from many other conversations we can have. This question is like an undercurrent, not always visible but always there and informing every prompt or invitation a spiritual director offers. The question is this, 'How is the dynamic of Spirit, Source, Love, God present in my life and what is my response?' You may talk about many things, from everyday life to your future dreams and the meaning of your existence. However, the question of my response to divine life is a centre of gravity which is always a reference point. The spiritual director will have an ear for the movement of the Divine, the whispers of Grace, the invitation to Life. In all of life, where is your path taking you, are you becoming more and more all that you truly are, all that your soul invites you to inhabit?

Beginning spiritual direction

You may be able to find spiritual conversation with someone you already know. Who do you talk with about things that matter? Start there and in due course you may find that you are looking for something more, and perhaps a little more distance and objectivity. The more honest you become in what you share, the more you might want to have those conversations with someone who is not part of your everyday life, someone who is not a regular friend or someone you see often in church or at work or around your friends. This distance means you do not need to worry what they think about you if you meet in another context. When you meet with a spiritual director, that time of an hour or so is completely sacred and you are free to tell the truth about whatever you want to say. If you are talking to a friend or acquaintance, you might wonder if they are surprised or disapproving, or even if they worry about your spiritual wellbeing. You cannot be completely honest if you are concerned about these things. Spiritual direction is like going in to a soundproof room – nothing you say goes beyond that space and in fact much of it will be forgotten when you leave. Not forgotten because the person was not listening – but forgotten because the spiritual director knows that this is just a moment in time, and when you speak again everything may have changed. So the spiritual director does not hang on to what you say, although the fact that they pay close attention will mean that they will notice patterns and themes which recur and they might mention these, so you can consider whether this is important.

If you do not already know someone you can meet with, there are a number of networks you can explore, such as lists of spiritual directors, which may be held by various organizations. There are some pointers at the end of the book which may help. Spiritual direction networks are usually ecumenical, which means they do not focus on one group. Church networks will not be limited to one denomination, such as Anglican, Roman Catholic or Methodist, they will include people from all kinds of backgrounds. Those who manage these networks will be able to help you even if you are not part of the particular church network holding the information. Some networks mainly serve the Christian community, others will be wider and will include people with a wide spiritual perspective.

Spiritual direction might be a time when you meet quite formally and sit together at a certain time and place you have agreed. Or it can be much more informal, a conversation over a walk or tea. Spiritual direction can happen spontaneously too. You might be having a general conversation and then the tone changes and goes deeper and for a few minutes, or maybe longer, spiritual direction is happening as there is listening and discerning. One way of expressing the heart of spiritual direction is the key question 'How I am encountering God and responding to God in my life now?' That conversation can happen quite unexpectedly, and this is one reason why many spiritual directors are uncertain about the notion that spiritual direction should be an accredited role. Spiritual directors are committed to good and safe practice as non-negotiable, but many take the view that there are ways to ensure this while preserving the tradition of spiritual direction as relational; undertaken with professionalism, but not over professionalized in a way that would narrow its potential and breadth.

Spiritual direction is not usually something people make a living from as their sole income, and such a model would not really be true to the nature of spiritual direction as traditionally understood. Spiritual directors are people who have time in their lives, alongside other occupations and responsibilities, to offer soul listening. However, they may have made time in their lives to offer this ministry and that will limit the time they have to work in other ways. Spiritual direction also involves some expense for the practitioner; they will have to pay for initial and ongoing training and supervision. They may also need to have insurance, which will protect them from the expense of defending accusations of malpractice as well as the expense of liability if someone trips on their doorstep and seeks recompense. These things are very rare, but the wise practitioner is aware of the potential risk factors, however apparently small. Charges for spiritual direction range from nothing at all to an unspecified donation, or an amount based on your income, or it may be a fixed sum. A competent spiritual director will tell you at the outset how they work so that you are not embarrassed by a lack of clarity. Spiritual directors are often people who have chosen to live modestly and frugally, they will not see spiritual direction as a financially-driven career choice. Charges are intended to enable them to live, rather than payment for services rendered. This may seem like a hair-splitting distinction, but in many churches clergy and ministers are paid what is called a stipend. This is not the same as a salary. A stipend supports you and enables you to eat and live, but it is not payment for your labour in the way that a salary might be.

When you make contact with a spiritual director, they will probably suggest an initial exploratory conversation. After that, either or both of you may feel that the necessary connection is not there, and this is not a problem. No spiritual director will be offended if you do not want to continue the conversation. If they say they are not sure they are the right person for you, don't take it as a rejection. A wise spiritual director knows that they cannot accompany everyone and sometimes their experience is too close, or too unconnected, for them to walk with you. Your soul deserves the most receptive listening space; this work is sacred and more important than personal preferences.

Spiritual directors have many different approaches, some will say prayers, light a candle or use Scripture. Others will ask what is helpful for you before establishing a set format. Think about what you need and what you are comfortable with. The person who accompanies you on your soul journey is there to encourage and support you so don't hesitate to share your perspectives and needs.

What should I look for in a spiritual director?

You may have a clear idea of what kind of person you are looking for to accompany you, or perhaps you have no idea at all and are looking for some guidance. The two main areas to consider are whether a person is competent, and whether they are the most appropriate accompanier for you in the light of all your current circumstances. You probably want to feel confident that a spiritual director will have some insight into your life and its challenges, as well as the issues you are wrestling with in relation to your spiritual path. Spiritual directors cannot have experienced everything there is to experience in life, and they will have a particular spiritual framework. Although their role is always to listen without letting their own agenda get in the way, it is not the case that you can talk to just anyone.

Spiritual directors will discern where their ministry lies, and they will not agree to accompany someone without knowing a little bit of background which will help them discern. You may have a sense that you would like to talk with an ordained person, or prefer someone who does not have a formal role in the church. Members of religious communities often undertake spiritual direction, and they often have a deep capacity for attentive listening, formed in a life of stillness and prayer. Age, relationships, family, work experience may all be important considerations, but try not to be too specific unless you are clear about your reasons. Spiritual directors are generally very open, and you may be surprised. In fact, someone whose life looks very different to yours may have unexpected insights. Trust the work of the Spirit; you will find the conversation your soul needs even if it takes a little while.

Competence and trustworthiness are very important, and you may be arranging to meet someone you have no previous knowledge of. Spiritual directors are trained to be very clear about the ways in which they engage in this ministry, and you should expect them to give you some straightforward information as soon as you are in touch and without you having to ask. They will probably tell you whether they have done a course in spiritual direction, and when and where it was. In the last thirty years the number of courses has grown, and it is unusual now for anyone to undertake this role without training. Exceptions might be those who have been doing it for many years and have learnt from their experience of receiving spiritual direction, perhaps in a religious community. These wise elders will draw on a life of their own spiritual joys and struggles, which they have talked over and prayed through over many years. Otherwise, you should expect a spiritual director not only to have done a course, but to be engaged in ongoing training and regular supervision, as well as having their own spiritual director. They will normally volunteer this information. They will also tell you whether they have insurance and whether they make a charge and what this is. They may give you some form of contract which sets out the expectations on both sides and covers what you should do if a meeting is cancelled. They should also tell you where they are accountable and who you can talk to if you have any concern about the behaviour of the spiritual director. It is very unusual indeed for such things to arise, but it is vital to have the processes in place and to know what they are; it will be too late if there is a difficulty later. The key thing is clarity; spiritual directors have different approaches to their particular boundaries, so neither side should make assumptions. Some will stick rigorously to a time boundary and will not expect to be in contact between meetings, others are more relaxed, treating the relationship more like a friendship. Neither is right or wrong, but it is important that you both agree how this will work. Don't be offended if the boundaries seem quite firm, this is necessary to ensure the effectiveness of the work and the well-being of you both.

Above all, look for signs that the spiritual director is on their own spiritual journey, there will be indications of this even if they do not tell you much about it. If you are unsure if it is going to work out, try meeting three or four times and see if trust and confidence are developing, it is not always easy to know from one meeting. Most spiritual directors will suggest that after a few meetings you take a gentle look at how it is working out, so that there is no reason for you ever to feel stuck in a conversation you are not sure how to extricate yourself from.

How to use this book

If you are contemplating finding a spiritual director or accompanier then you are preparing to enter into conversation about how Love, Grace, Courage and Compassion are moving in your soul and giving you Life. You want to listen to your soul, to tune into the God-space within you. But how and where to start? This book is a resource which may be useful if you wonder what you might actually talk to a spiritual director about.

INTRODUCTION

Listening to your Soul offers a number of short chapters, each on a theme, the kind of starting point that might frame a conversation with a spiritual director. The chapters deal with a range of everyday themes that everyone encounters. You do not have to take spiritual or religious themes to your spiritual direction conversation. It is best to start with your life as it is, with all the delight, hope and anxiety you may be experiencing. This is your reality, and it is the only place you can begin to look for an encounter with the divine, there really isn't anywhere else to go. Spiritual conversation is the conversation that happens when you are talking about work, or family, or anxiety, yet wanting to put that conversation in a bigger context.

There are many themes included in this book. However, it is important to recognize that they are all huge subjects in themselves and every one of them could be a topic for a major work of theology or philosophy. There are whole books about, for example, ageing, or work, or vocation. The purpose here is not to treat these themes in a comprehensive way, but to invite you to think about how these themes show up in your own life. Only you know this, and so these chapters offer a very brief overview which introduces the theme. You will know what it means for you.

Each chapter is in three sections. There is an introduction to the theme. This is intentionally brief because what really matters is your experience of this particular thread in your own life. An essay on the subject might be very interesting but it would not be about you and your unique experience. The notes will invite you into reflecting on your experience and all sorts of things will occur to you. You might write down some thoughts and questions as you go.

The next section in each chapter is called 'Preparing for spiritual direction'. It includes some suggestions for starting points as you think about your spiritual direction conversation. You might find one question is worth considering, and others are not relevant. There is no need to work through this material in a systematic way, it is not a programme of study that will lead you to a particular destination. There are prompts, and you can follow wherever they lead you. Start with your life as it is. As you tell the story of your life, practise listening to your soul.

Finally there is a prayer, or a prayer suggestion or pointer. These are deliberately short and might even seem quite perfunctory, which is deliberate. There are many books of beautifully written prayers available and you may own some. Prayers written by other people can be really helpful in articulating what our souls want to say when we can't find the words. We can use liturgy, words of Scripture, prayers and poems. Explore the ones that resonate for you and let your prayers be informed by such resources. However, the invitation in this book is to frame your own prayer, however halting and inarticulate. So the prayers are short and not necessarily poetic or eloquent. That is often what real prayer is like, so it is offered in that way rather than something poetic you have to try and live up to. Use these incomplete prompts as a springboard and pray in your own way.

The limits of spiritual direction

The themes in this book are introduced from the perspective of everyday life, with the expectation that any of these headings might be things you would like to explore in the context of spiritual direction. You would normally meet with a spiritual director about every six or eight weeks. You might meet more or less frequently for a matter of months, to accommodate a challenging period of one sort or another. The themes here are ones you are sure to recognize in your own experience. However, for some people these themes relate not simply to everyday ups and downs but to areas of woundedness and vulnerability. There may be things that are critical to the extent of challenging spiritual, emotional and mental well-being. If that is your experience, you will need more support than spiritual direction alone can offer. You may need to explore more deeply and find strategies for your life through more regular professional advice, support or therapy. This book offers only starting points for occasional conversation, and is not aimed at those who need therapeutic intervention to support emotional and mental health. If for example you experience loss or anger in relation to deeply traumatic and life-changing events, the overview here will not cover the ground you need. You may find spiritual direction supportive alongside other conversations, and your spiritual director will be careful not to cut across this work or undermine it. Some spiritual directors have experience of counselling, psychotherapy or coaching, but that is not a focus for the spiritual direction space. Such work has different boundaries and more regular meetings, perhaps weekly conversations. The pointers here may offer some threads to explore but they are general and invitational, and may not apply to particular challenges in mental health. If you are in deep distress, the kind of approach that would normally be helpful might not be right for you at all. Whatever your situation, it is important that you only make use of anything in this book that resonates. Not everything will; listen to your own soul and go where she leads you.

Spiritual direction is a context in which trust grows and often we find out more about ourselves than we expected. Sometimes this can become painful and challenging and can lead us to seek out more therapeutic help of a different kind. Don't be offended if a spiritual director gently suggests that you might consider counselling or therapy. They are simply being responsible and ensuring that they do not do more harm than good by stepping outside their own competence. Any such suggestion is likely to be very tentative and respectful, you can explore it together and come to a mutual discernment about ways forward. The most important thing at any point in your life is to think about what kind of conversations you need, where you can tell your story and what kind of perspective you need from someone else.

Preparing for spiritual direction

One of the wonderful things about spiritual direction is that every conversation can be new and fresh. Because you will not have met for a number of weeks, it is quite likely that life will have moved on and the topics and questions which seemed important will have either gone away or developed further. A spiritual director does not assume that you will carry on where you left off six weeks ago; that conversation might now be irrelevant. A good question to reflect on as you come to spiritual direction is 'Where am I and how am I today?' Notice how you are in your body, your mind and your soul. We are so distracted much of the time that we do not even really know how we are today.

If you really want to make the most of your spiritual direction conversations, which of course you will have set aside precious time for, and you may be paying for as well, it really does help to get ready.

If you keep a journal then in the days before you are going to meet, jot down things that seem important, along with any questions you are pondering. Think about where you will want to start, and consider what you would like from the conversation, what you would like to come away with. On the day, take your time to travel there and don't be in a rush. Do make sure you are on time, this values your time and the director's time, and most directors will not feel able to extend the time if you are late, either because they have other things to do or simply because it disrupts their day. It is good to know at the start of the conversation exactly what time there is, so if the director does not make this explicit, simply ask 'So how long do we have?' Managing the time should be a joint responsibility and you may find there is a clock where you can both see it.

In the days before you are due to meet, be aware of your soul state and note the threads you might explore. Consider possible themes and starting-points for a conversation. On your journey, take time to be focused and prepare some inner stillness. If you are driving, turn off the radio and consciously put aside thoughts of work or responsibilities. Think about where and how you will start. If you begin with a clear focus, you will use the time most effectively. You may not be sure where to start, and in that case just notice how you are and talk about that. Notice what you are carrying, what you are feeling, listen to your soul, give your soul time and space to be heard.

The following chapters are more like a recipe book than a manual. You can choose any theme that resonates with your life and experience, or you can work through the material methodically if that appeals to you. The chapters are not laid out in any particular order, there is not a progressive flow because it would be impossible to predict the path of any spiritual journey. The most important thing is to slow down and hear the questions in your soul and your body as well as thinking about them in your mind. As you read and reflect, notice where your heart sinks or lifts. Notice where your breathing changes and what minor responses occur in your body. All these things are clues, they are the vocabulary of your soul.

I

Hope

Hope is a beautiful word and carries so much. It means such different things at different times, and yet can be so elusive. As long there is hope, there is possibility, a sense that we are not in the hands of fate but that more than one path is possible for us. The absence of hope is a truly dark place because if we were to believe that there is only one path, leading to an inexorable conclusion, this would not be life-giving, not generative. Inevitability robs us of hope, of possibility, of tomorrow. If we are in the hands of fate then we are powerless. The insight that can move a person from hopelessness to hope is the moment of realization that there is still some shred of self-determination or empowerment to live from.

It is important to recognize the distinction between hope and hopes. Hopes may be future orientated, concerned with things that will come to pass or which we expect to emerge in time. We have hopes of so many things, for ourselves, for our loved ones, our longings and dreams. Our hopes are born of the desire that things will turn out all right, that our children will be happy and secure, that our lives will be peaceful, healthy, purposeful. We hope that certain things will go away, be resolved, or simply not happen. Hopes are often quite particular and may be based on evidence, or they may be aspirations or dreams. But we have a sense that we will know in due course whether they have been fulfilled or whether we must adjust to disappointment.

Hope, on the other hand, is not so focused on a particular outcome, it is more of an inward disposition, a way of looking. It is a lens, an attitude, a perspective. Hope is not the same as optimism. Optimism leads us to believe that things will turn out all right in the end, and this attitude may be due to an analysis of the data and the odds, or it may be a form of denial that refuses to face facts. But, like a list of hopes, optimism is largely concerned with outcomes, or at least that everything will be OK in a general way. Hope as a stance is not based on data, logic or information but grows from our spiritual or philosophical frameworks and values. Hope may spring from a deep belief that all will be well even though we cannot know how or when or even what that looks like. Hope may not imagine any particular resolution, it knows that what will unfurl may be something entirely unexpected. Whatever it is, we trust that it will bring life although we cannot determine in what ways or even for whom. This expectancy is neither denial nor calculation but a willingness to trust, to wait, knowing that life has a mysterious dynamic beyond our control. We are in the hands of Love, Life, Being, without guarantees, but with a sense of peace.

I notice how easily a vague mood of hopefulness can arise or dissipate, sometimes simply in response to what music is playing on the radio as I am driving, or because the sun has come out or gone in. That feeling may be no more than a passing mood, it is not really based on very much and it can be blown away as easily as it arrived. If our hope is rooted in nothing more than transitory influences, it is unlikely to sustain us when our foundations are shaken. The soul leads us into deeper waters and the work of spiritual direction helps us to negotiate them. When we listen to the soul's wisdom, we may find hope, and this poise will put all our lists of desires and hopes into a different perspective. We can keep them or let them go, hold them lightly or see them for the distraction they may be. But we will not over-invest in them or allow them to be a false guiding light.

In a spiritual direction conversation, you can explore both your hopes and your hope. There is nothing wrong with having hopes, we just need to keep them in their place. Hopes, dreams and plans can be highly motivational. You might start the conversation with thinking about the things you hope for, or the events you hope won't take place. From there, you can consider what really matters and what underpins your deepest wisdom, trust, peace and hope.

Spiritual direction is a place to tell the truth and to speak honestly about your deepest hopes. Sometimes they seem selfish, petty, insignificant, yet we feel them deeply and they are uniquely ours. It may be that some of our hopes are unrealistic or self-centred and we might learn to let them go. Other hopes might be things we do long for yet feel unworthy to receive. We might learn to give ourselves permission to desire things that bring joy and life to us, and let go of an image of a God who only gives us what we have earned.

Hope sounds like a future-orientated word but actually it's very much about now, the present, because hope enables you to rest fully in this present moment. There may be very real reasons why peace is elusive and the realities of life seem overwhelming. Nevertheless, in honest exploration and conversation it is possible to see more clearly how our hopes and fears, daydreams and longings are held in a bigger perspective. If you have a background story, an underlying narrative, which is hopeful, then you have a sense of connection and belonging which is powerful. It is hard to be hopeful when you feel isolated and alone. The very fact of sharing the journey with others enables hope to grow from the story of our belonging.

Preparing for spiritual direction

What are your hopes? Make a list quickly without censoring yourself. Take a piece of paper and write 'I hope …' at the top and list everything from 'that I can find a dentist soon' to 'that I might find friends who care for me'. Look at your list, what do you notice? Jot down anything you would like to reflect on in spiritual direction.

◇ When have I been most hopeful in my life? Do I recognize common threads about where I find hope?
◇ What undermines my sense of hopefulness? What have I learnt about myself?
◇ What are the things I believe about life, the world and God which enable me to construct a hopeful outlook?

Prayer

In moments of joy, I am thankful and amazed. My soul lifts, my heart sings.

At times of perplexity I wonder where I am, how it will be, what I might find and what might be lost to me.

Draw my attention to the immediacy of today with its gifts and realities, to celebrate and wonder but never to grasp.

Deepen my soul listening that I may find hope to live and to love in trust and peace.

When I am afraid, remind me that I belong to you.

2

Frustration

Frustration is a part of life, it is hard to avoid and it is certainly a reminder, as so many themes in this book are, that we are not in control. Perhaps not being in control is behind much of what comes into the spiritual direction space. We know we aren't in control, we know we can never be, and we even know that it would probably not end well if we were, but it is still frustrating. A spiritual director will hear the outcry 'I'm so frustrated' and yet hold the knowledge that there is a bigger picture. The current blocks are real, but beyond this narrow focus things will open up again. Frustration is often agonizing, because what we desire seems only just out of reach, only slightly beyond our grasp. The worst kind of frustration is when the breakthrough you want is tantalizingly close. Impatience is a close relation to frustration.

Frustration can be about blocks, delays, disappointments, inabilities to get things done. Frustration may arise because of other people. We focus on their apparent incompetence, stupidity, small-mindedness, laziness, personality failings, or all kinds of other apparent deficiencies and behaviours. It may not be individuals that are the problem but an organization or system, perhaps one that is dysfunctional, corrupt or broken, and this renders us powerless and marginalized. Frustration emerges when we are not in control of ourselves, other people, organizations, the neighbours or even our own bodies. We know what we want or need, or we think we do, and if the issues in the way could be resolved we could move on.

We love life to run to our agenda, our timetable, our priorities. Impatience and frustration are like twins, walking along together, telling us that things are not as they should be. Frustration and impatience feed each other. The more frustrated I am, the more my patience becomes exhausted. The less patience I have, the more I lose my sense of perspective and small irritations become bigger issues.

A patient spiritual director will listen to our ranting and raving until we are able to begin to tune into the wisdom somewhere in the soul which invites us to recognize that we can only be here, today. Tomorrow may be different, tomorrow things may be resolved, but until then we have to deal with how things are today. Today is all there is, all we have. Your soul invites you to take a look around, take stock, notice. As we do so, perhaps we will begin to notice where we are falling into panic, catastrophic thinking or anxiety. Sometimes we imagine that if we could fix the immediate problem we would be at peace and able to relax. However, we often find that this is simply not true. Frustration, anxiety and impatience do not just go away, they tend to land somewhere else. If I have a tendency to imagine catastrophe, as soon as the present impending crisis is averted I will probably focus on another situation which is causing me frustration.

In spiritual direction you can describe the whole frustrating scenario with all its twists and turns and complexities. Frustration is often the result of several things which would not be that hard to resolve on their own, but together factors create a vicious circle or logjam which we cannot unlock. The spiritual accompanier will believe you as you describe this. They will not tell you you are wrong to be frustrated, they are likely to have a lot of empathy, while at the same time encouraging you to find a way of looking at things which will help you move on rather than be stuck.

When we speak about frustration, we may express a lot of emotion, perhaps anger and tears. As we hear ourselves, we may notice that our voice might be just a little disproportionate or unreasonable in some small part of the story. We begin to recognize that while our frustration may be justified to some extent, it serves no purpose and does not help us to chart a course through. If anything, it gets in the way, distracts and paralyses us. If there is a way forward it starts here and not in some other place. In spiritual direction you may then recognize the small possibilities, the cracks of light. It is only when you accept where you are that you can chart the next step. It is not easy to give up feelings that we feel we have a right to hold, but when the feelings are blocking us as much as the circumstances, give them up we must.

Sometimes the best cure for frustration is to take a step back and notice where we have become intense and gone into tunnel vision. If the situation is not life threatening, and sometimes it really is, we might lighten up, see if we can smile at our impotence and fury. We might need to let go of the fantasy that we can arrange things to our own liking, in order to work out what the alternative is going to be and live with it. At other times we may need to take a breath and regroup to take on the practical aspects of the challenges we face. Your soul has a different perspective, a longer view; don't get mired in the detail. Sometimes frustration is not so much about our personal lives and problems, but about systems which need to be challenged in the name of justice and truth. Frustration may then be shared, and together you can work out a way forward.

Frustration, of course, may apply to anything from not getting the delivery we expected to fighting a huge unjust cause of some kind. When it comes to issues of global significance, we will experience far more than frustration, many other factors are involved. In those instances, we may have to deal with hundreds, even thousands of minor setbacks and frustrations as we inch towards our goal. If you are taking on a big project, there will be frustrations. Then, knowing how to manage frustration is vital, it will enable us to keep going, to maintain determination and resilience over months and years. Spiritual direction will support you as you dig deep, mine your resources. If you are going to take on a wider scenario you will need patience, fortitude and a sense of humour.

Preparing for spiritual direction

◇ What frustrations am I facing in my life?
◇ Where do I experience impatience?
◇ Where do I feel frustration and impatience in my body?
◇ What strategies do I have for managing frustration so that it does not paralyse me?

Prayer

God of possibility, freedom, peace, give me grace to rest in all that is here and now, however much this falls short of my desires and hopes.
I let go of agitation and impatience. I open my hands and my mind to a different perspective.
May I find courage to smile at my desire for control.
There will be time, there will be a way. Teach me to breathe more deeply.

3

Loss

Spiritual direction is a healing space to speak about loss because it is a place of listening. When you have lost something or someone, being listened to, being heard and believed, is vital. There is a wound in the soul, and words do not come easily. More than that, even when you find some words, they will probably seem inadequate to communicate what you really feel. There may be fear that when you speak, the listener will not appreciate the depth of your feeling. Perhaps they will minimize or rationalize things that are precious to you, or try to cheer you up by encouraging you to see some positive angles. Being told things might be worse, or that they might not be as bad as you suggest simply deepens the distress because now, as well as loss, there is misunderstanding and isolation.

When I speak about a loss I am in the midst of trying to process, I may feel as if there is a great distance between the words coming out of my mouth and the gaping hole in my being which is beyond all rationalization, modification, amelioration, or any other remedies my listener might be tempted to offer.

A compassionate listener is one who listens with their presence, their body, their soul. They do not burden you with attempts to minimize the loss, shift you into the future, count your blessings or offer other seemingly sensible or practical strategies. Sometimes these are helpful, but they can be no more than ways of avoidance or denial. Denial can have a place for a season, it may protect us from the full force of our emotions so that we can process a little at a time. A wise listener is one who does not try to force you out of denial but allows that space to give you safety for a time. Some listeners are able to hear stories of loss, yet others can seem almost desperate to shift you into a different place because your story is too uncomfortable for them to hear. At an unconscious level, someone listening might be thinking 'This could me be, so I don't want to believe it is really that bad'. In spiritual direction you should never have to be concerned about the effect of what you are saying on your listener. If you sense anxiety in your listener, you will hold back from saying more because it will not feel safe. A secure spiritual director has no need to move you out of where you are; they know that you can do that yourself if and when you are ready. Spiritual direction does not involve the accompanier trying to get you to some other place of their choosing. You map the journey yourself and sometimes that means staying in the same place for a long time. Your soul will know when you need to move on and your soul will let you know. Keep listening for the invitation, it may be very gentle.

In the midst of loss the only way you can think about it is probably the way you are already thinking about it. It is not at all helpful for someone to tell you to think differently. If it was easy or possible for you to think differently, you would have done that, and if there was a ready solution you would have already thought of it. Spiritual directors are careful not to underestimate the intelligence of those they listen to. You may have to rehearse the loss many times, from many angles. Spiritual direction is your space to do this for as long as you like. You may feel as though you were telling the same story again and again but in fact it will be nuanced in different ways as your soul wrestles, grieves, agonizes and maybe even rages. Your spiritual accompanier will let you do this, knowing that you are not being repetitive and you are not stuck. Once in a while they may say that they noticed something tiny, a change of tone or a different note. You may choose different words to express yourself. The spiritual director may simply draw your attention to this without suggesting it means anything in particular, or that it is a sign you are 'getting better' or 'moving on'. You can discern that when the time is right, but it may be reassuring to see that your soul is working, growing, finding new perspectives which can't be forced but which will emerge over time, perhaps a very long time.

Spiritual directors take the long view; they know that in their own lives they have spoken again and again to God, to spiritual companions of their own about their own soul and their particular losses, and it may have been truly hard. Your listener will be full of compassion and empathy, perhaps only expressed in their silence.

Spiritual directors know from painful experience the folly of impatience or being patronizing. They will take time to accompany you down through the layers of loss. This will not be endless, however much it may seem like it. There does come a turning point, a point when however overwhelming the loss is, it does not consume all your energy and time.

It is also important to bear in mind that a loss, even a small one, evokes feelings and emotions that really belong to many other losses, perhaps from a long time ago. If your feelings seem disproportionate then consider what other losses you might be carrying. Even a seemingly insignificant loss can put us in touch with feelings from long ago, events forgotten, dealt with by time and common sense. Yet what wounds the soul leaves a mark and sometimes that wound demands attention. This is the wisdom of the soul, a gentle reminder that perhaps it is time to give some love to some area of our lives which, for whatever reason, we previously ignored or moved on from too quickly.

Preparing for spiritual direction

◇ Am I carrying a loss right now?
◇ Are there losses from long ago which still feel tender and raw?
◇ Has a recent loss evoked feelings that belong to other losses?
◇ What losses would I like to talk about, simply to be heard?

Prayer

God, your world is marked by loss as well as joy. We know that many souls weep and rage for what was lost. There are things that have been taken from us, losses we did not consent to. Time and circumstance have swept some things away. There are those we hold responsible for some of the things we have lost. Some things are lost to memory and have been forgotten, leaving only sadness and grief. We have had to give up some hopes and come to terms with betrayal, bereavement and endings.
Hear my story. Help me write the next chapter.
In being heard may I find new peace.

4

Anger

It can be hard to talk about being angry, even to a spiritual accompanier who has given us space and time. Perhaps this is because so many of us have a sense that anger is in some way bad, unacceptable or dangerous. Think about the place anger was allowed in your childhood, in your school or home or church. The extent to which anger is acceptable can be due to a mix of cultural, generational and religious factors. In some homes emotions are expressed freely and they are understood as seasons which come and go, they are allowed to pass without too much comment. Previous generations may not have allowed the expression of anger, especially by children who may have been expected to keep quiet and do as they were told. Many older people will have had strict childhoods which allowed little place for the expression of feelings, or even thoughts and opinions. For some people, it has been difficult even to admit to themselves they were angry, never mind put it into words. If you have been taught that self-control is a particularly desirable virtue, then you may carry inside yourself an expectation that you might express yourself with calmly constructed and logical sentences and arguments. Without realizing it, you have internalized a judgement that calm is good and anger is bad. You might have heard the message that being angry is no excuse for being intemperate or emotional. This may of course be true, and unfettered rage is not always helpful. Nevertheless, at such times the focus may shift from the reason for anger to the shameful nature of being angry at all. This silencing can leave anyone, but especially a child, feeling silenced, misunderstood and rejected or judged.

When anger is disallowed by our internal censorship, or by

other people's judgement or power, it is then very likely that the anger will become a pot of fire in the soul, a pressure cooker of injustice and silencing. Many women, though not only women, have had this experience both in families and in their workplace. Children who have this experience lose confidence in their unique voice. We may wonder what is so terrible about being angry, and this is complex. In some contexts, anger is feared because it is an emotion that seems out of control and may lead us to say or do things that will be hurtful or harmful to others. This may include things that are said and later regretted, but anger can lead to physical violence too. We can be frightened by our own anger, and we can be afraid in the presence of anger. Ironically, forbidding anger is very unlikely to make it go away; it will simply go underground and feed on itself, perhaps to erupt in unpredictable, destructive ways.

Anger comes and goes; it has a nasty habit of being triggered, sometimes years later, by another event or conversation. It is possible to become angry about something long after the original circumstance, even if we were not angry at the time, consciously or otherwise. This happens when some new perspective, new understanding or new information arrives. We may realize that we had not seen the whole picture, or took too much responsibility for things. Perhaps we did not see how others were really behaving or how we thought too generously of their motivations. With hindsight we may conclude that perhaps we were naive or compliant and did not see what was really going on. This is not always a bad thing. It is better to think well of others as our default position rather than be cynical and suspicious as a matter of course. When we revise a story we had taken as read, it is a retelling, and the new story may be less comfortable. In order to protect our sanity and our soul, we may have told the story to ourselves, and perhaps to others, in ways that we could live with. We may have chosen to avoid versions of the story we simply could not bear. As deeper truth emerges we may recognize that if we had known or realized certain things at the time we would have behaved differently, said different things, expressed different emotions.

Think about what resources your spiritual tradition has to guide you at times of anger. The Bible contains many narratives about people who were angry – maybe you could have a meditative, imaginary conversation with one of them. A spiritual director can talk this through with you, and either do a meditation with you or suggest how you could do this at home later.

Preparing for spiritual direction

◇ What place has anger had in my life? Was I encouraged to express anger as a child?
◇ Am I carrying anger at this present time? Does it stem from unresolved things in the past or from current issues?
◇ Do I carry anger on behalf of others, because of what has happened to them?
◇ Where do I feel anger in my body? Can I notice it without judging myself?
◇ What am I really angry about – is it about the thing I think it is about or it is really about something else altogether?
◇ Can I think of a Bible narrative that involves anger? What insight or invitation does it offer?

Prayer

God, I am so angry, so angry it's hard to find words for the grating and grinding in my soul. Oh my soul, listen to this discomfort and seek to understand what it is really about.
Is this something I need to let go of or to put to use?
What threatens or frightens me? Am I confronting powers of injustice?
Touch my soul, Spirit of peace, in a moment of clarity, of independence. Draw me away from bitterness and into wise action and measured words. Where I am wounded, preserve me from the desire for revenge. Where I seek to protect others, give me wisdom to use my energy effectively.

5

Decisions

Different personality types deal with decisions in many different ways. Some people quite enjoy decision-making, others put off the critical moment for as long as possible and fear committing to a path that can't be altered. They fear 'getting it wrong' as if this was a bit like taking the wrong junction on the motorway. But life is not like a motorway, at least not in that sense. Life is marked by twists and turns, we loop back, find ourselves back where we started and experience dead ends, short cuts and diversions. Even these metaphors assume there is a destination in mind. The smallest decision is never insignificant, because something has changed and you can never really make that decision again. Even if you change your mind and do something different, the clock is never entirely reset.

Some personality types prefer logic and reason above intuition and others trust what just feels right and deal with what comes. Probably no one has only one approach, however; so much depends on the context. Some decisions have to be grasped, we have to move one way or another quickly. Other potential dilemmas resolve themselves and the decision is effectively made for us. New information, different feelings or a change of angle give you a different perspective. At some point the data is in and you have to decide.

If you are approaching a decision from a spiritual perspective, you might prefer the language of discernment to that of decision-making. Discernment is more than simply making a choice, it is about determining how to live, what to do next, which may be nothing at all. Waiting is as much a discernment as action. Discernment is less about what I want for myself and more about what is right, not only for my truest and best life, but for others and the world. What most reflects spiritual values, the glory and love of God, will be important in a discernment. The soul, if we have cared for her, is deeply in tune with these threads, sensitive to harmony, integrity and glory.

Our view of the universe affects how we approach decisions: we may believe that the world is generally a good and life-giving environment, trusting that even when things are difficult the underlying life energy is for good. We may believe that the universe is good, the gift of a generous God who has compassion for us and cares about our welfare, growth and good. Others are more cautious and believe that life is wild and raw, a jungle full of hidden dangers and predators. If that is your view, you will be constantly on the alert, looking for ways in which you might be tricked, disadvantaged or just unlucky. That is a rather exhausting way to live, and you are likely to become fearful and lonely. Spiritually mature people of any tradition don't seem to live like this, even though simple trust in life's abundance may seem childlike or naive to others. If you believe that every decision requires you to be streetwise, sceptical or cynical about others in order to negotiate misinformation or false promises, there will be no peace in the present. In the end, every decision is a step into the unknown and will have consequences we can never fully know about, foresee or understand. We explore this a bit more in Chapter 32 on choices.

Behind all our decisions are huge theological questions about how God acts in the world and in our individual lives. These questions are too big to unravel here, but ask yourself how you understand the ways of God. You do not need to work out the 'right' theology, just consider how you understand the ways of God in your own life. You might also consider the God you don't believe in, perhaps the God who is controlling and only has one plan in mind which you must find. Your theology will grow, develop and perhaps change, but where you are now is the context for your spirituality and your decision making. Your spiritual accompanier will accept whatever your theological framework is. If you are listening for the intimate loving voice of God to lead and guide you, you can talk about that. If that kind of relationship with God is not your experience or framework, you can explore the questions of guidance and discernment in ways that have coherence for you. The more you bring your decisions into your spiritual perspective, the more you will want to look at them in the light of a conversation with God, in harmony with an integrated view of God's world, God's love, grace and compassion.

Spiritual direction is a spacious place and you can take all the time you need. Your accompanier will not press you, in fact they are more likely to listen out for any hesitations or reservations that you might be choosing to ignore. If your listener senses that what you are saying does not actually express what is going on inside you at another level, they may gently draw you attention to this. They might invite you to think more deeply about where your inner dissonance may be. Spiritual direction can be a place to explore the hesitancy, fear or caution and let it speak to you. What is your hesitancy inviting you to hear?

All you can do is go the best way you know, for the best reasons you know. If you have regrets or doubts later, take these to spiritual direction. They don't mean you were wrong. Some would say that there are no right or wrong decisions. What matters is what you do at the *next* signpost. As you stand there and wonder which way to go, you will be informed by all the wisdom in your soul gathered from what has gone before.

Preparing for spiritual direction

◇ What kinds of decisions are on my mind at the moment? What is at stake?

◇ How do I see God as involved in these? How do I look for guidance?

◇ What are all the factors in this decision? Are there feelings or fears I am reluctant to name?

◇ What values are important to me as I consider a way forward?

Prayer

In my pondering and wonderings, I ask for wisdom to distinguish between fantasy and invitation, ambition and purpose, challenge and blind optimism. May I know your presence, God, in the depths of my soul. Give me courage to hear the uncomfortable things about myself as well as the startling potential for the creativity of new chapters and the life-giving energy of risk.

6

Prayer

You might have expected this book to be all about prayer, and in a way it is. There is an undercurrent of prayer in our souls all the time, a flowing stream of desire for Life, Love, God, which flows irresistibly back to the Source. We can listen in any time. As we wrestle with the complexities of life, this stream of soul wisdom and God connection is always there. God is in all things and when we approach life prayerfully that doesn't always mean we are saying formal prayers about everything. Rather, we are living in the knowledge that we belong to God, our every breath comes from a divine source of love and grace. This is who we are and how we are. We do not always need to talk about prayer any more than we need to be always talking about breathing. Sometimes we really need to pay attention to breathing, and sometimes we need to pay attention to prayer. At other times, both prayer and breathing continue faithfully and constantly, keeping us alive.

Prayer is in all the things that you talk about with your spiritual director, whether they sound particularly spiritual or not. Prayer is forged in the midst of all the things that take our energy and attention and love. The themes in this book are all very everyday things, and prayer is in every one of them. We learn how to pray not by reading books, though some may indeed be helpful, but by the experience of trying to work out what to say to God and how to listen to God every day. We are constantly connecting with God, with or without words, in all the joys, disappointments, worries, loves and despairs of our lives. This might be an instinctive 'thank you' or an anguished 'oh help' but this ebb and flow is ever present. No

PRAYER

one really learned to cook by studying recipe books, it happens
in the mess of ingredients as you touch and taste some very
particular thing. Cooking is not a thing without a context and
neither is prayer. Sometimes all we want in prayer is a sense of
being with God, held in love and grace. But even that does not
happen in a vacuum, it is in the midst of today and things as
they are that I seek that connection.

Prayer takes many forms and can be found in liturgies and
litanies, in sacraments and symbolic acts, in rites and rituals.
But a prayer is only a prayer when you pray it. The most beautiful liturgy has no life until it enters your soul and your soul
recognizes the prayer and prays through it. This is not necessarily an emotional experience, it is not a matter of feeling
spiritual or being noticeably moved. Connection can happen
without emotion or sentiment. The key with prayer is more to
notice when it is happening than to make it happen. In times
of silence, alone or with others, in times of shared prayer, we
are tuning into a mystery that is already happening. It might
be more helpful to talk about listening to prayer as our devo-
tional practice rather than making or saying prayers. The soul
is already there, in this life-giving stream of connection. Stop,
listen, attend and be a part of it. The soul longs to pray, and
as you listen to her sighs you will open the floodgates to overwhelming grace. Your soul knows how to pray, but she also
needs you to attend to the song so that the notes become strong
and vibrant. Listen for the song, listen for the harmony, join
your mind and spirit and body to the soul's prayer.

Preparing for spiritual direction

◇ What does prayer mean to me? How do I pray? How do I
want to pray? What is missing, if anything?
◇ How do I balance the prayer of breathing and being with
the prayer of intentionality and spiritual practice?
◇ What makes prayer difficult?

21

◇ If prayer is the natural language of my soul, how can I listen in and join in?

Prayer

Let me listen in silence to the prayer of my soul.
Oh my soul, teach me to pray, let me hear the song you are already singing within me to God, full of love and joy.

Write to God in your journal, or express your prayer in an artistic way with colour, shape, texture, sound.

Frame a simple prayer which you can repeat as you breathe or walk. Here is an example, but you can make your own.

O God
today is a beautiful day
all is well
today is a beautiful day
all is well
today is a beautiful day
all is well ...

7

Weariness

Of all the things the soul feels, weariness must be one of the most universally experienced. There is such a thing as spiritual weariness, which may be part of a more general sense of lack of energy, but it is hard to live with because there seems to be so little you can do about it. Physical weariness may lift after some rest, but weariness of soul cannot be remedied by trying harder, saying more prayers, or any spiritual exercise. Probably everyone experiences it, and you may feel too exhausted to even speak much about it. It is easy to abandon spiritual direction when your soul is tired and heavy, but this is the very time you might appreciate it the most. There is healing and life in saying how things are to someone who believes you and will carry a little of the burden with you.

Your spiritual companion will surely have their own story to tell, though don't necessarily expect to hear about it. But you may notice the compassion in their eyes, and you will have the sense that they have some idea of what you're talking about. They know that there is no easy advice to get through such times. No one chooses to be weary. It can creep up over time, developing from being a background feeling at first. Eventually we may find ourselves overwhelmed. It happens for many reasons, but it is usually a combination of things. Often in life we may be experiencing challenges in one area, yet at the same time there are other places in our lives which are energizing and offer space for renewal. When all the aspects of our existence seem to require more of us than we have to give, we can feel as though we are gradually being drained. Then, even the thought of prayer can feel exhausting. It feels like a dead end. Keeping going takes all the strength you have, and this means that things that would normally bring you delight pass you by. Life becomes a huge effort.

The most important thing when your whole being is weary is kindness, to yourself and your soul. Forget the demands, the oughts and shoulds, and let life be stripped back to what is doable. Don't give up prayer but in moments of desire and longing recognize the momentum towards God as prayer. Reduce demands and obligations and expectations to the minimum, there are usually some things that can be abandoned even if it means disappointing other people.

Listen to your soul when she is weary; even in weariness she has something to say. You may need to slow right down, make space, be in emptiness. But the soul has not given up, she is talking to you, asking for something, she needs you to hear her.

Preparing for spiritual direction

◇ Is there any weariness in my life at the moment? What triggers this sense and when does it dissipate?
◇ Does my weariness have a colour? Where is it in my body?
◇ Who is there around me? Do I need to recognize that I cannot navigate these times alone?

Prayer

Too weary to form a prayer, my soul is a desert unable to sustain or nurture me.
I ache through and through. The heaviness of my body reflects the weight of my soul.
I long to rest, to hide away from expectations, from all that is unresolved.
When I cannot form a prayer in my heart or my mind because I am soul empty, God, may I rest in your embrace.
Lay my head in a place of quietness and silence. May restoration and new heart flow into my body and soul.
Oh my soul, what deep wisdom are you offering me now?

8

Faith

Is faith something you have or something you do? It's hard to possess faith as if it was something you keep in a coffee jar. If you have it at all it's because it was given as a gift. Faith that is achieved, faith that we cling to like a lifebelt, is not something that brings freedom. Faith is more like a word that was spoken to you and which you received with tears of gratitude.

So often we think that faith is about believing things. These things may include teachings and doctrines, perhaps things that have been impressed upon us by the church as important. But even the resources of the church, or any faith tradition, cannot package everything up into a box that we can then accept as containing the essential elements of what we should believe. We may have many beliefs or perhaps just a few, but we have not got, and never will get, to the point of knowing and understanding everything. Faith will have some tent pegs, as it were, things that form the framework of our beliefs. But faith and beliefs are not the same thing. Faith and theology inform each other and in a growing spirituality this dialogue goes back and forth and both together inform life, relationships and actions. Beliefs are things we have come to accept as reasonably reliable. Faith does not mean that we take on beliefs in an uncritical way. Beliefs may be the content of our spirituality. Faith is what connects beliefs, life, prayer and action.

Faith is perhaps best described as connection. Faith is the thread that maintains the link between your soul and God. People sometimes speak about having little faith or a lot of faith or strong faith or no faith. However, faith is not necessarily something you can have in greater or lesser amounts. You might consider what the difference is between a lot of faith and a little. It takes a great deal of courage to act on what seems like a very little faith, so, as is often the case in the spiritual world, less may be more. We sometimes confuse faith with knowing or certainty. Faith is more about a sense of connection than a moral quality or achievement. There is no place in my soul that generates faith. It is given to me when I remember that I am not alone, that I am held, that I belong and my life has worth to God. If that is true then faith invites me to trust and I am able to say 'all will be well'. Faith holds me in peace when I do not know the outcome and I am not expecting any particular result, but I know that I belong to God. The soul naturally has faith; listen in and you will find it.

I don't worry too much about whether I have faith, I rest in what I have for today. It's like the manna that was given to the people of Israel in the wilderness, not something you can store and save for a rainy day. Faith is only for today, but you can certainly practise being open to receiving it. When hard times come I won't look in my faith bank to see how much I can cash in. I will ask that my empty soul can be open enough to see what is possible, receive grace, rather than be overwhelmed by despair. Despair is more opposite to faith than doubt. Doubt holds our questions and, although puzzled, it questions and wonders and this may feel uncomfortable. But doubt is usually not a fixed position, it waits for new light and is, at its most courageous, full of openness. Despair has nowhere to go, refuses faith, turns in on self and gives up. Despair says there is no path. Faith keeps walking even if the path seems invisible, non-existent or buried. The same is also true of doubt in its own way.

In spiritual direction, talk about what faith means to you and explore the ways in which you have felt you have had faith or lacked it on your spiritual journey.

Preparing for spiritual direction

◇ What does the word 'faith' mean to me?

◇ What beliefs do I hold dear?

◇ Do I sometimes feel my faith is weak? What would strong faith look like? What has challenged my faith? When has my faith been renewed?

◇ How might I be open to receive faith as a gift that connects me to God, others and the world?

◇ How has my theological understanding or my reading of Scripture changed my faith?

Prayer

Faithful God, your presence is constant, your creative
life infinite.
Soften my heart to receive the gift of faith that I may rest in
trust and joy.
When I am filled with despair, remind me that your
presence is life.
It is enough to belong to you.
Teach me to listen to the faith in my soul, where
complications and complexities do not hold sway. My soul
knows love, trust, hope.

9

Work

Work is more than paid employment. It can include a wide range of occupations, roles and responsibilities. Some of these are undertaken by choice, others are accepted as a duty or as a fact of life. That does not mean that the work is carried out unwillingly or ungenerously. Carers who have taken on the role for a family member may find themselves bound by a deep commitment to another, and this work is not always easy or well supported by others. This can lead to a great deal of conflict, since the commitment may be unwavering but the personal cost very high, perhaps unbearably so.

Attitudes to work range from loving what you do to feeling trapped by it. This may be the case whether the role is paid or not. Sometimes work happens because there is no one else and the task has fallen to you.

Spiritual directors probably spend a lot of time in conversations about work because whatever it is it takes so much of our time. Not having work is also a spiritual challenge. We may have lost it, given it up or be looking for it. These questions can consume much physical and emotional energy.

Occupations that have an element of vocation may seem on the surface a good way to live, because you are able to spend time doing what you believe God intends for your life. This may mean that your gifts and experience, your personality and your sense of call all come together. Nevertheless, work that is also seen as a vocation can be as challenging as any other work, especially if it does not live up to expectations for one reason or another. Perhaps exciting promises were made which have not materialized. Perhaps there are blocks to our dream work, such as difficult people in the mix, dysfunction in the organization, or financial concerns. Any of these can leave us feeling frustrated because 'if only' certain things could be fixed, all would be well. It is especially maddening if you have a sense of vision and long to be part of living out the Kingdom of God through your work. We don't always have much control over the work context we are in. Sometimes the circumstances are not negotiable, or it may be that we are accountable to others who do not have the same vision or priorities that motivate us.

Work may be a small part of life for some, but many people spend so much time at work that it has a huge effect on well-being, relationships and spirituality. In spiritual direction, you can tease out the issues about what the dynamics around work are for you. You might think about how best to live in your current circumstances as well as what you really want for the future. Work environments can be seductive. Little by little we may be mesmerized by success or status. For those pursuing a career, the possibility of more control, more money, more opportunity always around the next bend can be an ongoing lure which never really delivers. Most of us compromise in some way and success comes at a price.

Spiritual direction offers a context in which to explore which voices are really authentic. Some people take drastic action and walk away from paid employment to live on as little as possible. This may seem too extreme to be realistic for most people, but it is interesting that we find these accounts so engaging. The TV programme 'Lives in the Wild' allows us to go with the presenter, Ben Fogle, into the remote places some people have found in order to live an alternative life which is not dependent on employment or materialism. Perhaps some part of us will always envy those who walk away from the expectations and norms of the age. We can allow ourselves to be challenged without necessarily giving up everything. The characters in 'Lives in the Wild' may serve, at times, a rather prophetic function, demonstrating in extreme ways an invitation to live differently.

Sometimes it is a matter of life and death to leave work that is deadening your soul. When you know your soul will die of starvation and neglect if you stay where you are, you might risk almost anything to find a different way of life. Most of us do not need to change our whole existence to care for our soul, but if work is killing my soul I need to do something. If I cannot leave my work, I can pray for change, and I can look at ways of incorporating soul food into my life in other ways alongside my work.

Preparing for spiritual direction

◇ How do I spend my time? What place do paid and unpaid work have in my life? Am I content?
◇ What kind of explicit and implicit messages are inherent in my work environment about who I am, who I am becoming and what matters? Does this ring true for who I am called by God to be?
◇ What is the price I pay for the benefits of work?
◇ What changes might I want to make in my life to keep work in perspective?
◇ What gives me most joy in my work?
◇ Where does my work deaden my soul?

Prayer

In my work, whatever it is, I give thanks for all that brings joy.
I pray for those who I work with. I pray for generosity of spirit and for insight into the challenges others face which I might know nothing of.
Keep me from negativity, prejudice and boredom. Open my eyes to see possibilities for service and grace. May I enhance my workplace with kindness and care.

10

Sickness

Sickness is a very personal thing. We have to deal with our own as well as, sometimes, that of others around us. Sickness may be a brief inconvenience, a mere interruption, or an unwelcome visitor who takes up residence for an unspecified period, possibly never planning to leave. It changes not only our lives but our spirituality and may even affect our personality or, at least, the way we express ourselves. Sickness can make us fearful, short-tempered, impatient and angry. Even though we know this is happening we cannot always prevent it. Pain is distracting, debilitating and, even if we are thankful for medication, it rarely comes without additional effects and implications. In our vulnerability and powerlessness, we can feel overwhelmed and sometimes desperate.

We have very different attitudes to sickness, from worrying about anything at all to ignoring everything if we possibly can until we can do so no longer. Some sicknesses are disruptive but temporary, others we live with all our lives. Some change not only our quality of life but our life expectancy. These are very different scenarios, which will evoke different responses in prayer, yet there are theological foundations in our spirituality that will inform how we approach any illness.

Sickness can be very isolating because of the difficulty those close to us sometimes have in processing the circumstances. Family and friends as well as colleagues may say things that express their own agenda but do not really represent our own focus or priorities. Some will minimize what you are experiencing and, if this positivity does not really take account of the facts, it will be unhelpful. On the other hand, others in our world will appear to make a drama out of a crisis in ways that we are not. There are many reasons for the reactions of others and we are not in control of them, but people's reactions are often informed by their own fears or forebodings. They may have their own need to be reassured, and if a sickness is serious they may be wondering how they might deal with such a challenge themselves. All these factors and considerations can make it hard to have the conversation you really want to have on your own terms and framed by your own agenda. It is a strange thing that so many people around us seem to know more about what our bodies need than we do. We may be left feeling we would like more guidance from professionals and less from our friends.

In spiritual direction, the conversation will often turn to all the hopes, prayers and fears that sickness may have provoked. The scope of the conversation opens out to our relationship with God and what is happening, which is so much bigger than any particular issue. Sickness highlights all kinds of things, from self-care to life's purpose and questions about the future.

Spiritual direction, therefore, can be a welcome relief because you do not have to take any account of what your companion is thinking or feeling for themselves, in relation to their own life, spirituality or mortality. The spiritual director will take any such inner work to their own spiritual direction or supervision. You do not have to be concerned about them, and they are also more free to listen to you because they are not close to you in the way family and friends may be. In spiritual direction you can set the agenda, frame your own questions and express what is deepest in you.

In spiritual direction you can explore not only your hopes and fears, but how to pray. This is important because often when we are ill we cannot always pray in the ways that we are used to. We may not be able to gather with others, we may not have the energy or focus for our usual rhythms, and we may feel more distant from God and not know how to pray. The spiritual director will not tell you what you should do but will allow you to work out what will support you, give you life and enable you to connect with God, source of joy and hope.

Some of us, when we are ill, take the view that things will run their course. We trust in the capacity of the body to heal us, re-balance and renew as a natural process. This process may be supported and facilitated by medication, surgery, physiotherapy, psychological support, or all of these. We trust the work of God through the wonders of learning and science in the context of a holistic approach.

Others of us look for God to be very much more explicitly at work, perhaps in a way that appears not to reflect normal and natural processes and timescales. This is the world of the unexplained, perhaps miraculous. Throughout history, there have been accounts of ways in which people have experienced completely astonishing outcomes, even when a sickness appeared irreversible. Sometimes these miracles happen alongside medical intervention and sometimes completely independent of professional support. Some people will themselves have been part of church ministries offering healing prayer and will have experience of remarkable events in the lives of those they have prayed with and for. The spiritual director will be wise enough neither to dismiss these experiences, nor use them as evidence to support hopes that may not be realistic. It is vital to be open and hopeful, recognizing that even with all the scientific insight we have now, much remains a mystery. We need to avoid being gullible and consider all the possible explanations for a surprising turn of events. We can be cautious without falling into cynicism. There are many things we do not understand and cannot know. In the face of an apparent miracle the wisest thing is simply to be thankful. What is important is that we bring our own questions and prayers to God with honesty and trust.

Prayer for healing is a wonderful and life-giving ministry. It can bring comfort and peace and invite the power of God's spirit into some deep places of body and soul. The church has always believed and practised this. It only becomes problematic if particular groups begin to distort this understanding and use it to put pressure on people to 'have faith' or to suggest that a lack of correct response to God is a block to God's healing grace for ourselves and others. This approach can amount to superstition, or even spiritual abuse. If, in seeking prayer for healing, anyone is made to feel uncomfortable or unworthy then this is a very serious matter. People who are sick can be vulnerable spiritually and mentally; they need to be held securely by ministry which is accountable and adheres to the highest standards of good practice. If you experience anything that seems at variance with these principles, for someone you know or for yourself, talk to someone about it. You must be free to pray in your own way, from your own soul, without anyone judging your conversation with God. Any 'support' that elicits guilt, fear or anxiety is damaging to the soul. Your soul holds deep wisdom in times of sickness, listen to that voice. The soul knows that it can take time to recover well-being and will say 'Don't rush, don't let other people's anxieties and agendas disturb you.'

A spiritual director will take your prayers seriously. If you pray for God to work through medicine, they will not tell you that is limiting God. If you are praying for miracles, then they will be wise enough to have an open mind even if they have not experienced God working in that way themselves. In any case, it is not so easy to say what is or is not miraculous. The most important thing at such a time is to be heard, to be encouraged in your prayer. God is in all things and all things are connected. In this area in particular, humility is vital. Your soul will be your guide.

Preparing for spiritual direction

◇ What is my experience of sickness and how does this affect my relationship with God?

◇ What have I learnt about myself and about prayer in times of ill-health?

◇ How do I see God working in the world to bring health and healing? What do I pray for?
◇ What is the stance I hold in prayer? Do I pray from a place of anxiety or fear? Can I find a more peaceful place to stand?
◇ How does my soul minister to me when I am sick?

Prayer

My God, I was not looking for this sickness which is an interruption to my plans.
I wonder if you looked away for a moment when this happened to me.
I feel betrayed and let down by my own body, I trusted my body, perhaps took my health for granted. Is this a punishment for that?
God, I just want this all to go away, I want to go back to the time before this happened and I did not have all this disruption and worry.
Thank you for those who listen to me as I speak about my body and my soul.
Oh my soul, what wisdom are you offering me now?

11

People

Even if you are a hermit, there will be a lot of people in your life. They populate your past, present and future. We all have people who have in some sense stayed with us or inside us, even though we no longer have any contact with them. They belonged to a particular context, or we lost touch, or they may have died. Some will be people who have formed you, from childhood onwards. You will have significant memories of people who, by their attitude towards you, either helped you to grow or failed to nurture your confidence and development. There will have been significant moments that epitomize these relationships. You may remember the moment a teacher paid attention and took time to explain something, and how it left you feeling valued. This may have been particularly memorable if it was in marked contrast to your general experience of not being noticed, of being a body at a desk or a number on a register. That teacher is in some way still present in your life and perhaps you thank them now and then. Likewise, you may have the occasional word with those who did not notice or value you, who overlooked your soul. Long gone, they still exist in your memory. 'Look at me now' might be your challenge from the perspective you have years later. Again, these people are still 'in' your life because you carry them with you in some way. We are never really alone, with so many memories and experiences to influence how we feel about ourselves, others and God.

The introvert may feel as though their life is over-populated, and while able to celebrate the presence and gifts of others, they want to be left alone when at all possible. The more

extroverted may actively seek out a variety of voices and inter-
actions. Our lives are full of people, seen and unseen, real and
imaginary. These are the people who are in the room with us
when we talk with a spiritual director; we do not leave them
outside, even though we might wish to. As you sit down or
take a walk to have that conversation, you may be aware of
very many people in your space.

In the present, we are rarely truly alone because we are carrying with us all the people we currently need to engage with.
There are conversations being rehearsed or reviewed. We think
about the motivations, comments, actions and judgements of
others and we ponder our responses. All the time these people
are unaware of what we are doing, so we may be expending a
great deal of energy for no good purpose at all.

We have soul work to do when we are angry with someone, or when some precious part of our being has been ignored
or dismissed because a person does not fully recognize who
we are. When my authentic voice is not heard clearly. I can
feel invisible or drowned out. Spiritual direction is important because it is a space in which the people in our lives are
acknowledged in their proper place. We can separate ourselves
where we need to, distance ourselves from the unhelpful voices
and agendas and remember who we truly are. Other people
do not define us. If their assumptions, misapprehensions or
prejudice are simply wrong, we do not have to live in the light
of these any more than we would readily wear clothes which
do not fit and which we did not choose for ourselves. Another
person's perceptions of us may be informed by all sorts of
things which have nothing to do with us. They too have their
history, their inner voices.

Sometimes we need to place people outside our soul space
because their demands are too great or their agendas distract
and confuse us. Sometimes in a spiritual conversation we
become aware of the 'presence' or the 'voice' of others we do
not want or need in our space. Metaphorically, we can tell
them to leave the room because they are crowding our space
and diminishing our soul.

The spiritual director might ask who is in the space. Or they may point out that in effect there are those you have brought with you, knowingly or otherwise. Your accompanier will probably not know these people and will have no need to defend them or join you in being critical. You can tell the truth as you see it and talk honestly about your experience.

Preparing for spiritual direction

◇ Who am I bringing with me into the spiritual direction space? What conversations do I rehearse? Whose perceptions do I mind about?
◇ Who do I worry about? How much of my energy and resources does this consume?
◇ Are there those in my life who have caused me conflict? Are they taking up too much room?
◇ Who has wounded my soul?
◇ Who do I carry with me as I remember their love and blessing?

Prayer

Give thanks for those you carry in your heart with gratitude and affection.

Hand over to God those you do not need to allow into your soul space.

O God, give me wisdom to discern the ones who are friends to my soul, healers and lovers of my heart. May I welcome their presence and their voice, even when challenging. Give me the courage to close the door on those who clamour and threaten to crush my soul.

12

Exploring Ministry

If you are exploring a possible vocation to some kind of recognized ministry in the church, you may have been asked to meet regularly with a spiritual director. Those in formal vocation processes are encouraged, sometimes required, to have a spiritual director in order to have someone outside the process to talk with about the implications of the application and interviews. The process involves a lot of soul-searching and there can be frustrations along the way which need airing in a safe space.

A spiritual director can help you think through the practicalities that may concern you and, as they are not part of the process, you do not need to worry about how every comment or question makes you look. Licensed ministry, whether ordained or lay, is never just an individual or private matter. It is not a personal life or career choice that reflects your ideas and aspirations. Spiritual accompaniment will offer a context in which to tease out the threads and themes of what you really want to do, and why, and what the impact on those around you might be. It can be confusing to have on the one hand a clear sense of call, and yet on the other a whole series of difficulties or even blocks. What might God be up to? It is very common to find that a sense of vocation does not make sense, and we wonder if God has not thought it through!

Yet, as with so many of the themes in this book, so much flows from who you think God is and how God works. Does God mastermind our lives? Does the church always fulfil the will of God? It would be naive to think that whatever the church does or says perfectly reflects the will and purpose of

God. The process of calling people to ministry is surrounded by prayer and organized with a great deal of compassion and integrity, but it is nevertheless a human construction and sometimes it will not do perfectly what it was intended to do. It is clearly the case that there are people in ministerial roles who have not lived up to the trust placed in them, for one reason or another, or who turned out not to be really suited to the work. At the same time, you probably know at least one person who offered themselves and it is hard to understand why they were not 'successful'. The church does the best it can to discern and the Spirit works with what is. The hard part, though, is that we see the fallout from where the institutional process seems not to have worked. Spiritual direction is vital here, not least for those who feel that their lives might have taken a different course if the church had seen them differently.

It is very hard to process the confusion that can arise when your own sense of God's will is not confirmed by being heard by interviewers and selectors. Theologically, what do we make of that? Either God's will is being fulfilled and we must work with it, or the church has got it 'wrong'. Yet even if it makes 'mistakes', the church does not have the power, at the end of the day, to finally frustrate God's way. Spiritual directors will not offer this principle as a sticking plaster solution, but the conversation may in time restore hope and trust in the call of God. When God calls, this cannot be taken away from you, God does not need you to be formally recognized in order for you to live a life that reflects the invitation of God to all people. With God there is always another way. Always.

Spiritual directors are very familiar with questions such as 'What am I called to do?' 'Where should I go?' 'What is my life for?' 'How can I know?' and they will listen without anxiety. They know that although the way may not be at all clear to you yet, they have seen again and again that in the most surprising and unforeseen ways a path will emerge. The role of the spiritual director is to stay with you in anxious or uncertain and confusing times and not try to offer false reassurances that everything will be OK. No one can actually know this.

The spiritual accompanier will not make easy promises or unhelpful predictions, but within themselves they will be remembering that they have witnessed this unfolding many times. They recognize the territory, including what it feels like for you, and dare to believe you will find the path. They will have some insight into the excitement, nervousness and anticipation that comes with each stage. They will understand too the distress and frustration you may experience at times when there are setbacks, as there often are.

Those who have the authority to function as gatekeepers to particular roles in the church do not always get it 'right'. Even the question of what is 'right' is not easy. Some people believe that there is a particular path which is the ideal that God desires. Others take the view that God works in and through what happens and there is no one way that we have to fall in line with. We may start a journey with a particular destination in mind but along the way we are derailed by circumstances. It may be health, an institutional dysfunction or even global events. None of these are 'God's will', they just are what they are. The challenge in spiritual direction is to reflect prayerfully on what I have in this moment. In the light of what I do and don't have, I have to consider what my next vocational step might be. The spiritual accompanier may support you in taking very small steps, staying alongside as you wonder 'Whatever next?' and 'What does it all mean?'

The spiritual direction space will help you to stay grounded and focused, especially at times when the whole process seems overwhelming. Remember that a call to formal ministry is not a personal choice, you are responding to a call. That means that the church has responsibility for the process and for supporting you in it, managing the steps and inviting you to take each next stage. Allow this to happen, even when it does not seem perfect.

Spiritual direction is a safe space in which to speak of the disappointment, perhaps even hurt, when something you felt really strongly about does not seem to work out. It is also a good place to explore the complex responses of joy, amazement, humility and apprehension which may arrive when you are invited to undertake training or take on a particular ministry or post.

In all this, the spiritual director will keep you focused on your response to God. There may be some honest conversations, but also you will keep coming back to the centre of gravity, your open availability to God. Lift your face and hands in expectant and confident hope. God has named you and calls you and you will find the way.

Preparing for spiritual direction

◇ When have I experienced a moment of knowing that I am in the right place, doing the right thing, truly comfortable in my own skin, knowing my name and my place?
◇ What are the hard questions around vocation for me? Are there things that seem unresolved?
◇ How can I be open, available, expectant and joyfully confident? What gets in the way? What might be the next step towards developing an open spirit – without denying my difficult feelings or questions?

Prayer

God, I am following this path in obedience and trust, but I can't see where it will go.
Let me hear you call me by my true name, the name you have given to me.
May I recognize your voice and grow into all that you have named me to be.
I open my hands and my heart, my soul is waiting and longing for direction, but mostly to know that you are there.
Grant me patience and perseverance and may I discover joy.
Today, may I be a blessing to those around me and those I encounter as I express my belonging to you.

13

Vocation

Finding your vocation means discovering and living what you are really called to do and to be, in the place you are called to inhabit. You might understand that calling to come from God, in the context of spiritual faith. A sense of vocation might also be experienced as a flowing which comes from Life or Purpose, and this Life will be underpinned with values such as Love or Community. Perhaps Life is drawing you into a place of deeper engagement and commitment. The language of vocation is common not only in the church but also in contexts that are not at all religious or even spiritual. Vocation at its most functional can simply mean that it is to do with the match between who you are and what you have learnt, and how you live and work. Vocational training for a particular area of work may be juxtaposed with academic study. In that context it usually means that the learning is applied to some practical role or skill. Academic study that is not recognized as vocational is very important, contributing to a body of knowledge that may in due course have practical application. In the short term academic learning may be theoretical, gathering data and testing ideas. A vocational course in French is going to be more immediately relevant to a job in Paris than a study in medieval French poetry, though this of course may enrich my soul in all kinds of ways. We should never be quick to say that any particular kind of learning has no vocational application or practical purpose, you never know. For these reasons, it is wise never to dismiss academic study that does not seem to have an immediate application. It is also true that the study of art and poetry contributes to the well-being of human souls in all kinds of ways. Distinctions can be over-simplistic. Here we are thinking about vocation as finding a place in which you can be truly who you are made to be. Academics may be following their vocation as truly as anyone caring for others in practical ways.

Vocation is not a riddle or a puzzle that involves following obscure or cryptic clues. A spiritual director will encourage you to start with your life as it is. We are all called to live as human beings made in the image of God. That begins with simply taking care of ourselves, others and God's world. There is usually enough challenge in learning to be a human being, integrated and connected with the world, to keep us busy while we listen for some particular calling. You might explore in spiritual direction the nature of your deepest sense of self and purpose, and this will be more about who you are than particular tasks or roles. You cannot work out what to do until you have some sense of who you really are. A sense of identity, having a name that affirms what is in your soul, reminds you of your unique gifts and calls you to live in the light of your name.

To discover a meaningful sense of vocation you need to listen to your deep soul where this wisdom resides. However, this deep knowing is often buried beneath layers of life circumstances and the messages you have been given from various people at different times. Those voices are powerful and some people need more than spiritual direction to understand them and put them in their proper place. A skilled spiritual director will recognize when the conversation needs to go deeper into the relationships and experiences of the past to unlock something, and they will point you in the right direction without judgement. It is a wonderful thing, if sometimes painful, to begin to realize that some of the things we believe about ourselves are simply unfounded and originate from someone else's narratives.

Part of discovering vocation is discovering the freedom to find joy and liberation in your yes and no. That does not mean just being selfish and doing what pleases us. If someone asks me to put out chairs or do someone a favour with some transport, or if I am required to speak at a group, it is easy to say 'that is not my vocation' if I have decided that my only vocation is to write a book. But what about my vocation to be part of a community, to be kind, to bear the burdens of others? Putting out chairs may not sound like a vocation but belonging to a community and sharing the load certainly is. We do not have to live to the demands and agendas of others, but neither do we live in a private, self-referential bubble.

Discernment is a skill that develops over time, and the more you learn how to discern, the more you will be able to consider who you are, what is important and whether you are going to say yes or no. You will know why you have said yes or no, you will not need to defend or explain to anyone else, you will be at peace with either staying on course or changing track.

At the heart of vocation is the understanding of who you really are, and this cannot be limited to any one role, task or job. Your unique gift might find expression in many different ways of life, but underneath there will be a constancy, a thread that defines who God calls you to be.

Preparing for spiritual direction

◇ Take time in prayer to hear God call you by name.
◇ Do I have a name that God has given me?
◇ Can I live in the light of this name in my daily life?
◇ What frustrates my sense of vocation?
◇ Are there things I might do to express my deepest sense of call more fully?

Prayer

God, call me by my name.
Give me the courage and strength to live in the light of that name.

Thank you for the freedom of my 'yes' and 'no'. Keep me on track, let me be generous but clear, open but discerning. Remind me that I cannot be everything, do everything, have everything.

Help me to see that life invites me to be myself in so many ways. May I not wait for vocation to arrive, but see it in every encounter.

14

God

A spiritual director might ask you, early on in your conversations together, what the word 'God' means to you. It may seem like an odd question, but we may mean completely different things by this little, but not so little, word. So much is held in the name of God. For some, it is too holy a name to speak at all, and for others it slips out thoughtlessly or even profanely. It may represent some vague sense that there is 'Another' who is behind the universe in ways we cannot see or grasp, but which seem important.

Who is God for you? It will depend on your context and background and faith journey. For some, God is intimate, personal, close and present. The Christian faith tradition uses many relational words and metaphors. Father and Mother, Friend, Brother, are directly relational. Other words, such as Saviour, Lord, Logos, Sophia, Word, suggest an element of personal encounter with God, though their precise meaning and whether they translate into contemporary understanding can be contentious. The meaning of words is different in different contexts. If we forget this, we may confuse our modern use of a word such as 'Lord', to give one example, with what may have been understood in a different time and community. We use expressions such as 'to lord it over' which have negative associations connected with a particular culture. Translation leaps not simply across language but across generations of history, politics and social context. Although it is important to recognize these complexities, we are right to be cautious about simply deciding for ourselves who God is and what names we like. We might ask if a word that is offered by our tradition in a hymn or in the liturgy really expresses our theological under-standing of who God is and how God works. We do not invent God, make God in our own imagination. If we simply decide who God is on the basis of what we find attractive or accept-able then we remain at the centre of our world, self-referential. But at the same time we do not have to accept without ques-tion all the ideas that are presented to us. There may be more to encounter, more to discover.

The Christian tradition focuses on the Trinity, God as Father, Son and Holy Spirit. At the heart of this doctrine is relationality, connection, without which there is no life and no meaning. This Trinitarian formula underlies many prayers. The Anglican lit-urgy offers an alternative way of framing the Trinity as Source of all being, Eternal Word and Holy Spirit. This avoids the difficulty which some will have of naming God as Father with-out in the same breath naming God as Mother. Trinitarian language also has to grapple with whether we are referring to Jesus of Nazareth or Christ, the risen and eternal one. Jesus may be known as a daily friend and companion, guide and teacher, and for many there is a strong connection with Jesus the man who lived and taught in the world. Others will focus more on the Christ, Sophia, Logos, Word, and in prayer have a deep sense of connection with God as Creator, Wisdom, Source. The Holy Spirit too may be thought of in many ways. Images such as fire, dove, water and breath are helpful meta-phors. Often the Spirit, who infuses life with gifts and graces, is named as feminine, which may be helpful up to a point, but it is important to be aware of the theological implications. The Trinity is not made up of a male Father, a male Jesus and a feminine Spirit; God is wholly within and beyond each of these metaphors. God is everything and nothing. We need language and metaphor, but we have to recognize their limitations.

A key area to explore, often early in the relationship with a spiritual accompanier, is how you relate to God and the ways in which you think about God. The spiritual director will not want to be at cross purposes with you and will hope to frame a shared conversation in which there is understanding. They will be interested, whether they specifically ask or not, in what you mean by the word 'God' and what a relationship with God looks like. They may share something of the way they pray and tell you of their spiritual background and perspective, or they may not disclose very much at all. They will be trying to keep out of the way and not impose any frames of reference of their own – it is your point of view that is at the centre of the conversation. Perhaps they will invite you, from time to time, to explore, or at least consider, a different way of looking at things. In walking around your understanding and taking different viewpoints, you will understand your perspective more deeply, and add new insights to it as and when and if these are appropriate.

Preparing for spiritual direction

◇ What does the name 'God' mean for me?
◇ What language resonates for me in prayer, liturgy and in hymns and songs or poetry?
◇ What language do I find difficult to pray through? Are there words and concepts that are dissonant?
◇ Write a prayer of your own which names God in as many ways as you can, ways that invite and inspire you and heal your soul.

Prayer

Reflect on the many names of God you have encountered in Scripture and in your tradition. Take some time in reflective prayer to name God slowly and meditatively in the names that your soul offers you.
God, you have many names and none. I call to mind all those I know and as they fall away I sit with you as Silence, Namelessness, Being.

15

Belonging

Everyone needs to belong somewhere. Sometimes people will choose to belong, or at least stay, in a very difficult place rather than belong nowhere. The fear of moving on, leaving a place or community, can be very strong and may prevent us from walking away even when our soul is not flourishing. If someone says 'You belong here' and then puts up a barrier to prevent you from leaving, that is not belonging, it is imprisonment. Belonging is not about being physically with people or particular groups or in a specific location. Belonging is more about knowing where you are truly at home, even if you cannot live there or even travel there. Belonging is knowing you have a place, where you are accepted and welcomed yet at the same time being free, not being owned or coerced. You can choose to belong, or not, to a tradition, a community or a place. Others can tell you that you belong, and when that is an affirmation, a free invitation, it speaks of commitment and acceptance rather than barriers in your way that prevent you from entering in and staying. Think of the times in your life when a person or group told you that you could not belong with them. Sometimes that message is very direct, at other times it is subtle, implied. We have all been stung by being left out, not invited, not chosen. True belonging always has a freedom about it. Some people find pleasure in belonging to exclusive groups that are hard to get into for one reason or another. But there is something twisted about enjoying being one side of a fence which others cannot cross. True belonging is not enriched by keeping others out.

There may be people or communities or places that think you belong to them but perhaps you are not so sure. You may be able to say this and distance yourself, or you may need to hold a quiet inner poise that resists the assumptions of others. It takes courage to recognize you no longer belong in a place that has been a home, even a refuge. Somewhere that was safe is no longer the same, and to some extent that renders you a refugee or an exile.

There are places we want to belong but don't seem to be wanted, leaving us outcast or excluded. Sometimes that can be addressed, sometimes not, but in spiritual direction you can explore your true desires and speak of your search for home. The soul is precious and needs a home where the sacredness of your inner world is recognized as holy. The only place we can ultimately belong in safety is in God, but there are many people, communities and places that welcome us in love and grace and express something of God's embrace, if imperfectly. We cannot expect any person or group to offer us perfect belonging.

Belonging can be a fleeting thing, we don't have to belong in a place for ever. We may be a pilgrim, and sometimes this is more honest. There is a time to belong and a time to move on, a time to enter in and a time to travel away. Some belonging is part of who we are, it may be related to our ethnicity, our culture or tradition. Other belongings we step out of like clothes we no longer need. This is not easy for those who want you to stay, but listen to your soul, where do you really belong? Sometimes you have to leave a place of belonging to find a new home.

A curious thing about belonging is that we do not always know where home is, we may feel we are still looking. We may have never been there, but when we find it, there is a powerful sense of coming home. People who have left the place or community where they were born often have a strong sense of coming home on returning, even if they have no memory of their early life there. We are shaped and connected in more ways than we know.

The Kingdom of God is above all a place of belonging, a place to come home to. No one is turned away, no one is told they have no place at the table. In all our travels, our experiences of exile and wandering, this is a message of healing and hope. Your soul knows the way home, follow your soul wisdom.

Preparing for spiritual direction

◇ Where and when have I felt a true sense of belonging?
◇ When have I longed to belong and not been able to?
◇ How do I know I belong?
◇ Where are my places of belonging now?
◇ What does it mean to belong to God?
◇ Are there places I no longer belong? What is that like?

Prayer

God of home and hospitality, of eating and drinking at that table which is always big enough, may we hear your invitation with joy.
God of those who don't belong, who never belonged, who left, or who were cast out, remind us to be bearers of your unconditional invitation to come home.

16

Authenticity

When a person is described as genuine, authentic or real, we usually think this is a good and admirable thing. It suggests honesty and transparency, a confidence that what you see is what you get. An authentic, genuine person does not pretend to be anything other than who they are. They don't hide behind their capabilities, drawing attention to their skills or experience. Neither do they find their identity in their weakness as a way of avoiding responsibility. They are unafraid to present themselves just as they are, with gifts to celebrate and frailties to embrace.

If someone is genuine, then they aren't 'fake', pretentious or hypocritical. Their interest, their kindness, their help, can be taken for what it is, without fear of distorted motivations or cynical self-interest. They can be appreciated at face value and we know there are no hidden agendas. Authenticity includes showing the world honestly who I am, but it also means being true to myself. People who are authentic know, love and accept themselves and are comfortable with all that they are. They don't see the need to compete, judge themselves harshly or get things out of perspective. They aren't driven by fear and insecurity. Authentic, genuine people can speak from what rings true in their own soul. Sometimes this is not comfortable for others to hear. There may be an element of being prophetic when people speak out of the heart of what they know to be true to themselves and to the Kingdom of God, regardless of popularity or even one's personal safety.

If you are going to tell your story to someone and trust them to receive it graciously, compassionately and generously, it will be important to you that the person listening is indeed who they seem to be. Often, spiritual direction is a place where we go to try and find a more genuine and authentic way of being and living. I may talk to my spiritual director about the challenges on the way to being truly authentic. It means listening to my deep soul and considering who I really am. A careful spiritual accompanier will be tuned in to the things we say which express our soul, and will notice the things that don't ring true, the things we are taking refuge in. The conversation can highlight and make space for the things we hardly dare articulate about ourselves, our identity, our hopes, our longings. 'Say more' is often the invitation in the conversation and the spiritual director will give you space to stay with the theme, follow the thread. If your spiritual director is silent, it may be that they are giving you space to keep going, without interrupting the flow and diverting your attention.

Discovering how I can be authentic is always going to be a work in progress. It is many layered, and we do not always realize how much we are not being true to who we really are. It takes courage and the love of others to live authentically. The power of community can make a difference here too. As we learn to accept others and value their gifts, we trust they will do the same for us. For spirituality to be authentic, it needs community in some form.

Being authentic is costly, it means that I have to consider more joined-up thinking in the areas of my life that don't add up. I say I believe one thing but don't always follow through with my choices. It is easy to notice the speck of inconsistency in someone else's life and ignore the log of hypocrisy in mine. Becoming whole is the work of a lifetime, taken in small steps. What matters is whether we are growing, or diminishing and disappearing as our true soul is lost and silenced. Authenticity is perhaps rather like humility; if you think you have it, then you don't. It is visible only to others. Your soul knows when you are not being authentic because soul cannot lie or deceive. Soul invites you into becoming all that you really are and can be, whole, integrated and utterly authentic.

Preparing for spiritual direction

◇ What does my soul tell me about who I am?
◇ Where is there dissonance in my life? Are there things I can do about this?
◇ Does my desire to be authentic draw me to speak or act in ways that are uncomfortable or costly?

Prayer

Jesus, as you lived and loved, as you laughed and wept, did you have to learn who you were? Did you agonize over choices and possibilities?
Your compassion came from deep within. Your anger was fired by love and passion for justice and truth.
When I forget who I really am, remind me of your life, your words, your clarity.

17

Failure

Everyone fails sometimes, it is an inescapable part of being human. Failure can be embarrassing and humiliating, we feel exposed and vulnerable. Perhaps our first response is to look for a reason, an explanation that will take the sting out of it. If we can see what went wrong we might feel less useless. It may be that we want to blame someone or something, a natural reaction but sometimes bringing only temporary relief.

When something seems like our fault, we often shift from thinking about a thing that has failed to the idea that we ourselves are a failure. We can move very quickly from the experience of one project that misfired to concluding that our whole life, personality and competency are under question. We may then be consumed with self-recrimination and regret. If those close to us try and comfort us and minimize our mistakes, we may think they are just being kind but wrong and our distress deepens. We wish things were otherwise and if we had only done or said certain things differently we would be in a different place.

If something happens that is just unfortunate, that is not failure, it is life. But when we set out to do something and it did not come to pass, then we feel responsible. Sometimes we have to accept that responsibility, learn from it and put it down to experience, Sometimes we have to see that it may not all be down to us and be a little kind to ourselves. A gentle listener may help us to do that, treading the fine line between accepting our genuine sense of failure and looking for a kinder tale to tell. Failure is humiliating because it seems that the whole world can see I messed up, miscalculated, fell short, dropped the ball, did not deliver. I could have avoided this, but I failed to see the signals, change my course, see the evidence. Failure may lead to shame and that too is something that goes deep into our souls.

We can take this sense of self-blame to spiritual direction, knowing that our accompanier will not be superficially quick to soothe but neither will they collude with our backward glance or self-pity. In spiritual direction I can tell the painful story but begin to look for another chapter. Perhaps some things can be put right, perhaps not. Perhaps I will have another chance and nothing will be lost in the end and I will have learnt a lot. Or perhaps an altered course will be found and, although it will not be what I planned, it leads to life and hope in its own way.

When something difficult happens, we come up with a whole range of narratives, we may have many versions of the story. We may move from thinking it is all my fault to realizing that this is not so. Alternatively we may want to blame everything and everyone initially, and only as we find security can we begin to acknowledge the part we played.

The spiritual director will not judge which narratives are true but give you space to evaluate every perspective. Every version of events will have some elements of reality and some blind spots. In time a balanced and nuanced understanding emerges. I can accept responsibility but also seeing the complex factors and events will find a sense of perspective.

Failure may lead to forgiveness, for myself and for others. When we accept our own frailty we cannot be less generous with others. The spiritual director will accompany you through this conversation too, never rushing but always inviting further exploration when a new thought emerges.

The soul is kind, does not condemn, invites us to forgive ourselves. Take time to allow your soul to offer you peace.

Preparing for spiritual direction

◇ What failures sit heavy on my soul?
◇ Where do I carry the regret of foolish actions, words or choices?
◇ What story do I tell? Is it the whole story?

Prayer

With you, God, success and failure are not categories to
define life.
Our dead ends become corners to turn round and discover
new paths.
Our disasters become new themes in the story.
Broken threads are woven in, backward glances
become wisdom.
Give me humility and courage to tell a new story.

18

Identity

Have you ever woken up and for a split second not remembered who you are, where you are or anything about your life? It is a very strange moment and quite a relief when the pieces fall into place a moment later. Your life does not seem like the sort of thing you would forget easily.

Spirituality is one expression of the realization that I am not at the centre of everything, there are other points of reference. This concept is the starting place for all spiritual exploration and practice.

If I am not at the centre then is there an ultimate reference point? Even if we say that is God, we will need to think about what we mean by that. When I know that I am not at the centre, the ways in which I am perceived, named, encountered, understood by God, others and the world are questions asked from a different and freer perspective. We all have many roles and relationships that give us a sense of identity. We may reject these as representing things that other people have imposed on us. Part of growing up is to understand that we do not have to be defined or limited by what other people have laid over us like a cloak of expectation or obligation.

Spiritual direction offers a context in which to explore the everyday challenges to our sense of identity. When we are secure we are less easily offended or slighted. This does not mean we don't need to challenge the insensitivity or ignorance of those who don't recognize our identity, but it does mean that our voice will become one of education rather than retaliation. The expectations and obligations melt away as we discern how to live as our true selves, express friendship and faithful service with joy and integrity. When we encounter stereotypes and prejudices, our first response might be to become furious and resistant. When we feel invisible, our soul is bruised and we may feel we have no presence, no voice. We are at our strongest and happiest when we do not need to wonder if the projections of others might really be true. When we are secure we are able to see the illusory and deceitful nature of projections and prejudices and we can refuse to take them into our souls. We are free to recognize who we are and who we are not. The spiritual director helps us to puncture illusions and claim our true identity, including our frailties and wounds. We can know how God names us, and that name is whispered to us alone, no one else hears that healing voice. There is no need to live in a box constructed by others. If we are rejected when we refuse to take on an identity constructed by others, we can remember who we are in God's eyes.

Some people explore tools such as the Myers Briggs Personality Type Indicator (MBTI) or the Enneagram in order to understand and develop their self-awareness and self-understanding. There are many other systems, questionnaires and ways of categorizing who we are. The MBTI highlights our preferred ways of functioning and helps us to understand what energizes us. The Enneagram invites an understanding of the ways in which we are often motivated, without realizing it, by fears and insecurities. When we are able to let go of these and see them for the illusions they are, we can live more freely, generously and joyfully.

Our soul knows our true identity and is always drawing us gently back in that direction. Some of the inner conflict and dissonance we experience in life is because we are trying to be someone else. We do have to adapt to other people, it is part of being human, but the ways we adapt can be compassionate, self-aware and mindful. I can choose to meet someone's expectations of me, because that is the right thing to do here and now, not because I have to. At other times, I can step back from those expectations, clear that I am not responsible for what others demand of me. There are times when we know that to save our soul we have to withdraw, make time and space to heal our true selves. At such times, it is important to listen to the urgent prompting of the soul as she invites us to spend time away from expectations, perhaps alone. In the silence and stillness review the journey you are on, consider where you are not free to be yourself and consider what might change.

Preparing for spiritual direction

◇ What shapes my sense of who I am?
◇ What expectations and obligations have been presented to me?
◇ What are my feelings about how others perceive me?
◇ How might I live more truly from the person God knows, names and calls?

Prayer

O God, I am fearfully and wonderfully made,
You know my name and it is precious to you.
Remind me who I am in you.
Give me courage and grace to be all that you call me to be.
Give me patience and compassion when others look past me or through me.
Teach me to see others in all their beauty, give me ears to hear their story, told in their own words.
I open my heart to your invitation.

19

Joy

Spiritual direction is definitely about joy. Sorrow, bewilderment and spiritual pain are sometimes real and important starting points for the conversation, but spiritual direction is not intended to be a problem-focused ministry. Joy springs from thankfulness, which is key to spirituality. Gratitude means I look beyond myself to see that whatever is good and bringing joy in my life is a gift, I probably did not make it happen all by myself. You do not have to believe in a God who is 'he' or 'she' to be thankful. Thankfulness may simply be recognition, acceptance that somehow Life has blessed us and we know not how or why. In moments of deep appreciation it is natural to breathe the words 'thank you, thank you' from some inner place we are not always in touch with. In these prayers, for that is what they are, we acknowledge the love, grace and creativity that comes from God. We are lifting our gaze to the Source of life and goodness, knowing that it does not come from us. It is a deeply human instinct to say 'thank you' because we know that life is so mixed, comes with no guarantees, and moments of joy are treasures to cherish.

Joy is like an underground stream in our lives; sometimes it flows deeply and we know it is there, but it is hidden, perhaps so deeply that we cannot hear it at all. When joy hides from us we press on in trust and faith. Joy may be elusive, she does not appear at our command, but a little goes a long, long way. A moment of joy can sustain you for weeks, months, and even after years it will not be exhausted. Joy sometimes emerges in the most unexpected places, and your conversation in spiritual direction will help you to be ready, keep listening and watching for signs of life. When joy bursts in it can be truly immersive, a soaking as tangible as hot sunshine breaking through clouds. In that moment all we can do is lift our faces and be thankful. Where does joy come from? Sometimes it just seems to appear, a gift out of almost nowhere. At other times you have to mine for it, commit to its reality and simply believe in it. Joy can never be forced, it simply refuses to be coerced in that way. But I can open my hands a little, soften a little, lift my face and stop scrunching up my eyes so much. Joy is more of a disposition than a feeling. It's a place to place myself, a gift to receive, a guest to welcome, one I can't make appear according to my timetable or my agenda.

The absence of joy, joylessness, is a particular kind of emptiness. It is flat, like compacted soil which is unable to support life because there is nowhere for roots to penetrate and find air and water and nourishment. Inert and flavourless, hopeful of nothing. Silences that appear to hold no promise are hard to bear. Yet in music a silence is a pause that enhances the whole. There are pauses in the midst of birdsong or a moment between the ebb and flow of waves. We know from experience what these pauses mean and what they promise. We know the song or we trust the orchestra. We know that the rustling of leaves in the wind is not a constant sound but rises and falls moment by moment. The still of the night is deeply alive, yet there are long periods of deep noiselessness. These pauses may invite us to hopeful waiting, but when we are without joy this may not seem possible.

There are vicious traps in the midst of joylessness and however low we may be, we can ask the spiritual director to help us look out for them. We may be drawn into despair, self-pity, self-indulgence or negativity. These places might seem entirely justifiable, but they can draw you in and seduce you with a kind of dark comfort and oblivion. Bitterness is never a good place to settle. Spiritual seekers are never satisfied with despair. Spiritual life that is authentic is never self-focused, so even in the midst of despair there is an invitation to look up, out and beyond.

The absence of joy has to be acknowledged as a reality that everyone experiences. The hardest times are when you lose sight of the undercurrent of joy which has always been there, however far beneath the surface. You can teach yourself to notice joy, allow it in, catch it in flight, taste it, perceive its fragrance.

In times of joylessness, hold your nerve, look up, wait. Spiritual conversations can help you to notice joy, find it and be available to it. The conversation is a place of solace when there seems to be nothing to notice and no way of being available to joy. A spiritual accompanier both listens to the emptiness of joylessness and also delights with you in moments of joy. A spiritual director will notice what effect joy has on your soul and they may invite you to wonder how this gift will be transforming and healing. However, they will not insist that every gift of joy has to have 'meaning' or be applied in some way in your life. Joy is unconditional, free, simply to be savoured. Joy builds resilience and hope in your heart, resources that will be another gift for another day.

Being open to joy is a spiritual practice. It is part of breathing. It may take a bit of effort at times, but the more we are open to joy the deeper our capacity for it becomes.

The soul craves joy, longs for it so much that she will find it against the odds, in unexpected places. Keep listening to that longing, follow the trail to the source. There is joy to be found for the thirsty soul.

Preparing for spiritual direction

◇ What experiences of joy are most memorable for me? Can I still draw on this gift of life and energy?
◇ What ordinary things draw me into a place of joy – is there a way to make these part of my spiritual rhythms and practices?
◇ What robs me of joy? Is there a way of guarding my inner joy?

Prayer

God of joy, laughter, thankfulness, slow me down that
I may find the joy I so easily miss in my distraction
and anxiety.
Teach me to live in the light of the knowledge that joy
will be found when I least expect it.
Remind me to breathe gratitude again, and again,
and again ...

20

Endings

We are not always very good at endings. Often we pretend that
they are not really endings at all. Even death can be minimized
as not really much of an end, its finality softened with emphasis on what continues. This is not necessarily wrong, and we
will say more about that particular ending in another chapter,
but life is filled with endings of one sort or another. Spiritual
direction is a place to reflect on them, their significance, what
they mean to us and how we might process them. Some endings call for celebration; they may be a point at which we are
released from the expectations and obligations that we have
held for a season. Whether we are moving house, leaving a job
or resigning from a group or committee, the ending may mark
a change in roles and responsibilities in a helpful and healthy
way. Some endings are very clear, but at other times boundaries may become confused and we may have to ask whether
we have really ended as completely as we need to. Perhaps we
cannot bear to let go, or maybe others will not release us. The
spiritual director is sensitive to the words and the emotions
and the dissonance that may be evident when we talk about an
ending but will indicate that our soul is still present to what we
thought we had left.

When we are free, secure and our soul is not clinging to the
past, we can say goodbye to whatever has come to an end.
There are things we are glad to end; other things are taken
from us by age or circumstance in ways we do not choose or
even foresee. ,

It may sting a little when other people are more apparently
brutal about endings than we are, but there may be wisdom

in the recognition that a chapter has drawn to a close. Some friends, colleagues or acquaintances do not even pretend that the relationship is likely to continue but make a more or less clean break. This may hurt, but at least it is honest and may reflect that person's previous experience, their fears or wounds. Keeping something alive which has run its course often means that the ending will be drawn out, unsatisfactory and messy. There may be a mismatch of hopes and expectations and an eventual drifting, so that only later do you realize that there was in fact an end but it was not named, acknowledged, celebrated or grieved.

Spiritual direction is a safe place to anticipate endings and consider how they might be lived through. Even where we have little control, there is inner work to do which enables us to be at peace with endings of various kinds. Some will be huge and life-changing, others are perhaps temporarily dramatic but will find their perspective as we move on.

Spiritual direction conversations themselves also come to an end. Some people talk with the same accompanier for many years. Others meet just a few times or maybe just once. Discernment and honesty are required by both people. A mature spiritual director will usually recognize when there needs to be a change. There might be many reasons for this and they will have thought carefully about it and probably taken the question to supervision. It does not mean that they do not care, in fact it demonstrates that they care enough to get out of the way. Circumstances may have changed and a different emphasis or tone is needed which you need to find elsewhere. A spiritual director will not keep meeting with you indefinitely without reviewing from time to time, and they will have the honesty to tell you when perhaps your conversations have run their course. If this is the case, they will not end suddenly but there will be conversation, possibly over some months, and they will want to ensure that you do not feel abandoned.

Perhaps you feel that the conversation has completed the work you needed to do. Don't hesitate to share this, a competent director will not be offended or feel rejected. Some people look for a different spiritual director when a very significant chapter in their life comes to a close. There may be a feeling that there has been so much focus on one particular chapter that what is needed is a new conversation in which those particular issues are not 'in the room' as things that you have shared a lot about. A new spiritual director may well learn of this period of your life, but it may be important to you that they were not 'there' in the same way as the person who accompanied you at that time. When a spiritual direction relationship ends, you may feel that you are leaving behind some aspects of yourself you have now grown through and away from. A spiritual director will be glad to review the journey and support you as you discern the way forward to deepen and develop your spiritual life further.

At times of endings, listen to what your soul needs. There can be a complex interweaving of emotions; take time to recognize the threads and the untidiness.

Preparing for spiritual direction

◇ What endings am I negotiating now?
◇ Have there been endings in my life which were unsatisfactory or unresolved? What gifts or wounds have these left for me?
◇ Have there been times in my life when I needed to say goodbye to myself as I was?

Prayer

God of beginnings and endings, God of the ceaseless patterns of seasons, of light and dark, of gifts given and joys surrendered, teach me to celebrate memory, growth and even loss. Teach me not to cling. Free my soul to journey on with a light heart.

21

Dreams

Dreams are endlessly fascinating, though they may seem so ridiculous that we may feel self-conscious talking about them. We may wonder what another person will make of them, and yet at the same time we want to tell someone. We may need to share the bizarre tale and see the funny side of it, or we may be troubled and need some insight, or at least reassurance.

We should neither make too much nor too little of dreams. People engage with them in different ways, and this will depend on where you believe they come from. On the one hand, dreams are a perfectly natural and necessary function of our minds and bodies. Apparently everyone dreams, although some people will not remember them; they fade without us having any awareness of the way they are de-toxing our minds. We may be more conscious of dreams at times of anxiety or stress.

One way of engaging with dreams is to understand them as a way of God speaking to us. For some, this is fairly direct, God gives us the dream and it will contain either a very obvious meaning or something we have to discern, perhaps with the help of others. In the Bible, there are many stories of people who experienced God speaking through a dream to warn or guide. Another approach is the belief that God works through our God-given natural processes to invite, warn or reassure us. This middle way means that we can receive our dreams as part of our spiritual life and relationship with God, without necessarily seeing dreams as dictated by God without any input from our own lives. God created minds and bodies that have some incredible capacities for deep knowing, and much of the time this passes us by as we engage with life on a superficial level. To listen to your body, to the unconscious, is to listen to your soul.

Sometimes our dreams reflect the desperation of our minds and bodies to draw our attention to those things we are trying really hard to ignore or deny. We may be struggling with stress, conflict, fear or memory. These and many other factors inform our dreams while we are busy choosing not to listen in our waking hours. It may take months of recurring dreams before we begin to ask the soul what she wants to tell us.

Some dreams are probably just the mind resetting and we would be foolish to try to read deep meanings into everything. We might be alert, though, to patterns emerging which might draw our attention to themes in our lives. How do we tell the difference between a significant dream and one that is just the result of everyday processing? Listen with your whole being. There is often something about the quality of a 'meaningful' dream which lodges deeper in our body with a sense of 'I am not sure what this is but it seems to come from somewhere deep within.' As you wake, there may be the sense that you have been offered something you need to attend to, even if you cannot even remember the dream very well. Details will often surface again in those waking moments if we stay with the elements we recall. Once the connection is lost, it may be gone for good, but one image can be a thread that allows the rest of the dream to come back into focus and be recalled in detail.

If you have nightmares or your dreams leave you traumatized, you will need more support than spiritual direction can offer. Dreams do a lot of healing work on their own, but sometimes they tell us that we need to ask for help. The mind and body may be in pain which cannot be resolved in the normal process of sleep and rest. Your spiritual director will support you if this is the case and the spiritual direction conversation may continue alongside the help of a skilled therapist.

Recurring dreams do not necessarily mean that we have unresolved issues, it may just be that we have a 'favourite' dream our minds use when we are under pressure of any kind. Many people dream about exams, even into old age when academic pressures are a distant memory. The dream is not about exams at all, but it is a familiar metaphor which evokes similar feelings of being assessed, not having time or failing. Our dreams are influenced by our background, culture and experience. If passing exams was considered a measure of worth in my childhood, exams will serve a similar purpose in my dreams, telling me I am worried about not measuring up in some area. Someone else will have other images and metaphors. This is why it is wise to be cautious about universal dream meanings, where particular animals or motifs carry a particular significance. This may be interesting, even informative, but in the end no one can tell you what the horse or elephant in your dream really means. In the Christian tradition, interpretation usually comes from discernment and insight rather than reference to symbols. The connection, when you identify it, will ring true in your soul and that is the voice you need to trust rather than schemes or systems for interpretation.

You can talk to a spiritual director about a dream. If you are not sure how they will respond, you can ask 'Can I tell you about a dream?' They are unlikely to say no, though they might warn you that they do not have any expertise in this area. That does not matter, you simply need a good listener. Some spiritual directors are interested in dreams and may suggest a particular process, such as repeating the dream in the first person and in the present, for example, 'I am walking down the street and I see all the shops are closed.' This takes you back into the experience of the dream with all its images and feelings. As you replay and review the dream, you will notice things that you had forgotten or not thought important.

Spiritual directors will not try and interpret your dream for you, that is a dangerous way to go. As they listen, they have a different perspective, and they may spot a connection you have missed. However, they will offer this observation very tentatively. It might be an 'aha' moment or it could be completely distracting. Your accompanier will impose nothing but will encourage you to find wisdom by deepening your own listening. You can do this by slowing down, paying attention and perhaps rehearsing the dream a number of times to see what different threads emerge.

There is no doubt that dreams are soul work, and attending to them deepens that work. Sometimes it is enough that we had the dream, we simply need to trust that the soul is doing what she needs to do. We do not always need to make any more of it. At other times there is a powerful moment of connection between a dream and your present life, which can be challenging, humbling, uncomfortable, perhaps even humorous. We realize what we have been up to and in the light of that realization we can discern what, if anything, we need to do.

Preparing for spiritual direction

◇ Am I aware of my dreams? Do I want to make an effort to remember more? How might I do that?

◇ Are there repeating dreams which present me with familiar themes? What does this feel like? Is there anything unresolved which might need my attention?

◇ How do I distinguish between the dreams you need to consider and those it is not necessary to obsess over? What are the signs of an important dream for me?

◇ Do I have a way of processing dreams? Do I write them down?

◇ Talk with your spiritual director about what dreams mean to you.

Prayer

God of dreams and dreamers, you speak to us in the night through our minds and imagination. Teach me to trust my body, my soul.
Remind me to take time to listen to the stories my dreams tell, to embrace the surprising invitation to wonder. May I allow my dreams to offer wisdom and healing.

22

Scripture

For Christians, the Bible is a sacred book of stories, narratives, history, prayer, prophecy and poetry. It includes the Hebrew Bible as well as the Gospels and Epistles that emerged from the early church. Its long history draws on many traditions, oral and written, over an extended period of time. We can never take the Bible at face value in a simplistic way because even the work of translation involves interpretation. Languages do not have matching, equivalent words and ideas, and even for those who can read Scripture in Hebrew or Greek there are many questions of nuance and context. We have to consider the differences in culture, context and community. Furthermore, what does it 'mean' and when and for whom? We have to think about the layers of meaning Scripture has. If we can come to understand what an author intended for the community they wrote for, we will have valuable insight, but the message for a different community at a different time cannot always be quite the same. The challenges, questions and circumstances will be different, although we may find many common threads and themes. We may find that theological principles have an utterly and radically different application for a different generation. This does not mean that we play fast and loose with Scripture; it challenges us again and again to hear what it says for us, not someone in the past or the future but right now.

Such questions are way beyond the remit of a book on spiritual direction, but it is vital to recognize the importance of this textual work. Your spiritual life will certainly involve reference to sacred texts and you will need a framework for understanding what they are and are not, what they can and cannot offer you. Sometimes when people begin a course of theological study they are confronted with questions that had never occurred to them before. This can be frightening to begin with, but usually turns out to be liberating once the student is secure in the knowledge that the Bible is still the Bible. Layers of meaning have become apparent; this deepens our engagement with Scripture and reminds us that we are engaging with living texts, not merely ancient ones with no currency for our lives now.

A spiritual director will not tell you what approach to have to Scripture, but they may invite you to think more deeply about how you listen to the text and what you expect to find there. You might want to think about how you understand God to work and speak through the words of the Bible. Sometimes Scripture speaks to us very personally and immediately, the words leap off the page as if they were meant just for us. When this happens, it is wise to stop and pay attention. Don't let the moment pass, if you try and come back to it later you may find that the sense of immediacy has vanished.

Think about what your approach to Scripture means to you and talk it over in spiritual direction, especially if your perspective is changing in some way as new angles present themselves. Perhaps it is important to you to study the texts and place them in historical and theological context. Such exploration can inform and deepen faith. Others engage with the text just as it is and allow it to speak simply and directly without necessarily researching all there is to know about it. There is nothing wrong with this, as long as you understand that you are approaching it for yourself and therefore you may not appreciate all the nuances of context and language. You may find in due course that questions occur which you want to follow up. Studying texts is a way of prayer, and so is simply sitting with the words. One way of doing this is the practice of *Lectio Divina*, a quiet and meditative openness to perhaps one phrase or word, savouring it and allowing it to enter into your soul.

There are many kinds of sacred texts and many religions have a holy book. Spiritual wisdom may be found too in writings that have never been designated as 'sacred' in the way that the Christian church is clear about what does and does not belong in the Holy Bible. The Apocrypha is included in some Bibles, placed between the Hebrew Bible and the New Testament. The Christian tradition includes different views on whether these books should be included as Holy Scripture, and some believe that these writings are important and useful, but not necessarily sacred.

The Bible includes texts that were not originally 'scripture'. They found a place in the community over time and when first written may have been essays, narratives, prayers or letters. We should not be surprised then to find that God speaks through poetry and art and music just as engagingly and powerfully as through verses of the Bible. If you are arrested by a poem or sculpture or picture, engage with it as a window into God, just as you would with a text from Scripture. God's spirit is not limited to the words the church has formally embraced.

We have been exploring Scripture here, and for many that will mean the Bible. Notice, too, how other texts may speak to us and hold a challenge, an assurance, as powerfully as the words of the Bible. A poem can be God's voice, God's word, God's invitation. You can practice *Lectio Divina* with poetry or spiritual writing and allow every word to soak into your soul. This does not need to be religious poetry, any writing can connect us with God, God's world, our deep self, and take us into prayer.

Preparing for spiritual direction

◇ What place has Scripture had in my life? What do I believe about the ways it might inform my faith?

◇ What spiritual disciplines shape the way I read sacred texts?

◇ What aspects of Scripture trouble me? Talk this through with your spiritual director. It can seem 'wrong' to be critical of things that we read about which we find shocking or not consistent with trust in a loving and compassionate God. Be honest, search for understanding.

◇ Where do I experience God speaking to me through poetry, art or music?

Prayer

Choose a verse or a single word of Scripture and sit with it for a while as a focus of reflection and prayer. Don't think about it or analyse it but allow it to enter your soul.

Today, I will be open to the possibility that a poem, a painting, a sculpture or piece of music might speak directly to my soul.

I offer my soul to be transformed by God's word, wherever it is found.

23

Darkness

A book about spiritual direction would hardly be complete without some consideration of darkness as an experience of the soul. Dark times are part of the human journey and the Christian tradition. The night service of Compline takes us into the darkness beyond sunset and is a reminder of the perils, spiritual and physical, that we may encounter when we are asleep or vulnerable. Night comes to refresh, heal and renew, but it is a time of not seeing, not being able to hurry the dawn. One of the most famous writings in the Christian tradition is *Dark Night of the Soul*, from the pen of the sixteenth-century Spanish mystic, St John of the Cross. It is a poem of longing and love which came out of great suffering. It is often quoted and frequently misunderstood. The dark night as John understands it is not simply a low time or temporary, superficial depression, but something much more soul-searching and profound. St John describes a life-changing spiritual experience which had the effect of deepening further his devotion and passion for God.

Whether or not we go to the kind of depths St John of the Cross experienced, we will certainly not avoid times of darkness, and these may be inner trials, invisible to others, or they may be times of trying life circumstances which bring spiritual challenge, or both. Sometimes we have no sense of God's presence. Yet at other times the darkness is an experience of God. God is revealed in darkness and in light, they are not opposites. Light can be so dazzling as to darken our vision. Darkness can be filled with Presence and Glory. The spiritual director is likely to have had their own journey of darkness but they probably will not tell you about it, and may not even make any reference to it at all. They know that your path is different and at times of darkness it is not always helpful to hear what someone else went through. That is their journey and they navigated it in their own way. If you are climbing Everest, a map of Snowdonia will not help you however beautiful it may be. There will be few, if any, points of connection and even if there are superficial similarities, this can be misleading. There is no reason to think that what someone else did, or how they prayed, will be the right path for you. Your path is uniquely your own. Spiritual directors probably won't tell you what you should read, how to pray or how to get through. But they will listen out for signs of how you might be finding a path, they will encourage and affirm you.

The story of the road to Emmaus in Luke's Gospel (chapter 24) is a very well-known account of a journey from one place to another on foot. But when the disciples arrived with Jesus at their destination for the night, they soon found themselves setting off back to where they started, entirely changed. They had been in despair, they thought all was lost and that their hope in Jesus had been a foolish delusion. Then with the breaking of the bread, Jesus is recognized and this new insight changes everything in a moment. The end of the dark night may come suddenly, with a revelation, or we may creep our way out over months or even years. But we emerge changed, with a different perspective and nothing is the same again. The disciples retraced their steps with joy; we can imagine that the return journey, which may have been in the dark, was much quicker than the first. They have travelled through darkness and light and are back where they started.

Preparing for spiritual direction

◇ What does a dark night of the soul mean to me?
◇ What have I learnt from dark night experiences?
◇ What keeps my longing and desire for God alive?
◇ How do I experience light in darkness?

Prayer

I thank you that you are God of darkness and light,
both alike to you.
You cannot be diminished, silenced or banished, your
Presence and Glory are not contained.
In the midst of what seems dark, I know your light.
In your brightness I cannot see you. Teach me to go by
the ways of darkness and light, to be drawn by love not
by sight.

24

Disappointment

Disappointment is an odd thing, and often we feel it more keenly than we are prepared to admit. Perhaps that is because if we admit to wanting something very much and then being really devastated when it does not work out, we fear we might appear in an unflattering light. Things that are deeply important to us can be very personal; I may not want others to know just how much they mean to me. Perhaps I am applying for a job or finding a place to live, and I am working on a plan that seems just perfect. Even if we do not believe in superstition, we may inwardly have a sense that we might jinx things if we get too excited. But whether we have emotionally invested or not, the scale of disappointment can be surprising. A door closes, a dream has not been fulfilled, hopes are dashed. Disappointment can be a crushing experience and although we may soon pick ourselves up and move on, it can feel overwhelming for a time.

One way we deal with disappointment is to rationalize and tell ourselves it was not really that important. Or we think of all the downsides and pitfalls that might have resulted if we had had our way. Alternatively we may try and 'spiritualize' events by wondering what God's will is and whether God was in it, or if God had a better plan. The spiritual director will gently help you to tease out these questions so that your theological thinking is robust and considered. Fatalistic or superstitious thinking is not good theology.

We can be disappointed with God, with ourselves, with other people or just life. Even things over which we have no control at all, such as the weather, can disappoint because we hoped for something different. This of course is completely pointless, and we are wise if we remember that, as we cannot control the weather, it is probably best to be prepared for all possible outcomes and not pin too many hopes on something that may or may not happen.

Listen to yourself describing your disappointment to a spiritual director. They will not judge you and they will recognize the depth of what you feel. The pain of disappointment is not always proportional to the reason, perhaps because it is often complex. We may feel guilty for expressing disappointment if it seems to reflect selfishness or perhaps a lack of trust or faith.

Disappointment is part of being human. It is better on the whole to be optimistic in our approach to life than pessimistic and negative. To hope for the best is a life-giving attitude as long it does not involve negating real concerns. We might need to adjust our expectations.

At times of disappointment, the soul is a refuge, the soul never disappoints but will remind you of what is really important, will renew hope and perspective.

Preparing for Spiritual Direction

◇ Where in my life might I set my heart on things I have no control over?

◇ Have I set ambitious goals for myself or others? Are they realistic?

◇ Have I been disappointed with God or with what God has given me? Have I longed for God to speak or act and been met with disappointing silence?

◇ Where do I need to acknowledge the sting of disappointment in an honest way?

Prayer

I give you, God, the sharp sting of my disappointment.
I know it may pass but for now the sense of crushing,
the nausea, is real.
This is one chapter, there will be others. God of endless
possibility, imagination and creativity, I will give thanks
for what I have, what I have learnt, who you have made me.
I begin again.

25

Creativity

Some people express their prayers in creative ways, which might mean making something tactile or visual, or enjoying music, language or metaphor. Creative writing can be poems, essays, reflections or novels. Prayer can flow through the joy of cooking, baking, sewing, gardening. As your spiritual life flows, you will long for more and more ways to express the life and love within. The soul that is alive resonates with all creation and delights in all of it, from urban architecture to birdsong to mathematics or movement. Anything and everything can be a means of articulating a connection with the divine life.

Spiritual directors love to see people grow and discover new ways of prayer. You may not have thought of crochet or designing a garden as prayer, but it really can be. Part of the reason we lack imagination around prayer is that our image of God is too limited. If we imagine that God is essentially interested in religious activities then we will keep trying to pray in quite churchy ways, with overtly religious resources. Prayers and liturgies and practices certainly enable and enrich prayer, but there is more. Planting a seed in a pot of compost can be as much a prayer as saying words from the prayer book. My hand holds the seed, recognizes it as gift with potential for life. The earth is damp and soft and ready to receive the seed, to nurture fragile roots and give life. How is this not prayer? Growing things remind us of our connection to all life, and this movement is prayer.

The spiritual director will gently encourage you to see that more and more of your life is prayer, recognizing the prayerfulness in everything that you do. We do not have to be creative in religious ways for our efforts to be prayerful. We may imagine that painting, calligraphy or quilting is somehow more prayerful if the subject is religious. But writing out a verse of Scripture in beautiful script is not necessarily more prayerful than a practice sheet of one letter, repeated many times. When it is done with attention and love and joy, it is prayer. When we recognize these simple things as prayer, the prayer becomes conscious, intentional and therefore deeper, and we are led into spiritual encounter which is vibrant with life.

Many people think they are not creative at all, but often what they mean is that they cannot draw or make things. But there are many ways of using colour and shape and texture, as children do all the time. Children enjoy the process of creating, adults tend to focus on the end product. We can also be inspired by the creativity of others in words or images. A simple photograph can offer a new perspective, or a poem can invite us to understand ourselves more deeply. Take opportunities to gaze, to touch, to use all your senses and celebrate beauty.

Creativity feeds the soul, whether you are engaging with the beauty or challenge of the work of artists, poets or musicians or playing in your own way with shape, colour or sound.

Preparing for spiritual direction

◇ What creative activities do I enjoy? What seems to come easily, or what would I love to learn?
◇ What holds me back from developing confidence in some area of imaginative expression?
◇ Could I be motivated to give time and discipline to practise a skill or art?
◇ What small next step might I take?
◇ Where could I go to be inspired by the creativity of others?

Prayer

God of shape and texture, sound and colour, energy
and beauty, surprise and invitation, remind me to play,
to invent, experiment and wonder.

26

Disorientation

Disorientation is a feature of spiritual life. We get lost again and again. Fortunately we are also found again and again. God, who never lost us anyway, reminds us of where we belong and holds us in grace, which is exactly where we need to be. A new path opens and we set off again with new vigour. We may move through this pattern many times.

Just when you think you know where you are, the ground can start shifting. It often starts with a niggle, something does not quite fit as it once did. A question emerges and the answers we receive from those around us are just not convincing. Or possibly something very sudden turns our world upside down and we know that we will have to recalibrate.

When we are disorientated, for whatever reason, our trust in God may be shaken and rocked. Imagine taking a familiar path, suddenly to find that nothing is recognizable and the signposts, if there are any, don't make sense. Things that were reference points now cannot be relied on to point the way, locate us or serve as markers. It is frightening when you cannot interpret your experience, you cannot work out what to do next or which direction to take. You do not know what to trust.

People often come to spiritual direction for the first time as a result of some kind of disorientation. It may be because your understanding of your faith is being re-evaluated and your theology or spirituality is taking a new direction. Perhaps there has been upheaval in the church you have belonged to, or your places of belonging are no longer secure. Changes in relationships, work or home can unsettle us. The solid ground underfoot no longer feels safe. It is unpredictable, shifting.

The disconcerting thing is that the people around you do not necessarily share this sense of dislocation or movement. For many of them, things are just as they have always been, so they may seem impatient or frustrated with you. You are asking questions that have never occurred to them. They may try to help but their suggestions do not get to the heart of the matter. Meanwhile, you cannot rest. The questions are real and seem more urgent with every passing day. To begin with you may think it is just a phase and things will settle down. But eventually comes a turning point, you must leave familiar ways and places and beliefs and shape new ones, or wait for them to emerge.

Spiritual directors recognize disorientation because they hear a lot about it. They know that you are speaking the truth and when you say you did not want this to happen, they believe you. The spiritual director will enable you to understand that when we travel we sometimes get lost. If we stay comfortably at home we will never lose the path, but we will miss a lot. Our world will be narrow, self-referential and uninformed.

A spiritual director can remind you that when you are disorientated this is something written about in the spiritual tradition. For Christians, the Psalms are a resource for prayer and reflection. They describe the joy of being close to God, the despair of feeling cut off, and the experience of hanging on in trust until the relationship is restored.

Being disorientated can be isolating and lonely, you can feel judged and misunderstood. You know you are not being difficult on purpose, nor are you ungrateful. You have simply lost a sense of being anchored.

Disorientation is part of a cyclical pattern, and it is reflected in the seasons, in the church, even in the daily rhythm of night and day. It is a dynamic that leads to new insight and growth. In the midst of a disorientating experience we may feel lost and stuck, but it is in fact a sign of movement and growth. Disorientation resolves, whether gradually or suddenly, and we will find ourselves in an entirely new space, enchanting and compelling, full of wonder and new possibility.

Preparing for spiritual direction

◇ When have I become disconnected from beliefs or communities I thought were home?
◇ What experiences caused me to question things I thought I knew?
◇ What sustains me through searching for new understanding?

Prayer

I don't recognize where I am, God.
The familiar has become strange. What was once reassuring now raises questions and uncertainties. My soul is restless.
I am confused, yet I know I had to find another path. No longer at home, I had to set out on a journey, but no one wanted to come with me, I feel alone.
Speak lovingly to my soul and remind me that I am not truly lost, that this path will turn another corner and lead on to a new place, a new journey, a new sense of direction.

27

Sleep

Sleep might not seem like an obvious thing to talk about in spiritual direction, but it is deeply connected to spiritual life. We can't function without sleep and yet we often behave as if factoring it into our lives is something of an inconvenience. Wakefulness can certainly be a spiritual experience, perhaps of prayerful wrestling or of deep peace. It may allow for focused intercession for others in ways that don't seem to happen during the working day. But sleep at its most restorative is a time when our minds rest and our souls are at peace. When we lack sleep we become physically and spiritually exhausted. We may become emotionally fragile, over-react and feel out of sorts with ourselves and everyone else. We become more vulnerable to illness of all kinds. When our bodies are asleep, all kinds of processes are happening in our cells, to repair, renew and regenerate. Our bodies wait for sleep, to attend to the processes that cannot happen when we are awake and dealing with immediate stresses and demands. Falling asleep, we trust that in the hours to come our body is engaged in these healing processes, which are outside our conscious control. If the hours intended for sleep are restless, fitful, disturbed, the work of healing and renewal is disrupted. When we do not sleep well, we will soon find that our body and mind will find many ways to tell us to rest.

A spiritual director is not a sleep therapist, but you can certainly talk about sleep from many angles. If you are well rested, notice what patterns and habits support this and make sure you continue with rhythms that support you. Many people have what is called a Rule of Life. This is simply a structure for your life which takes account of all the patterns and rhythms that support your spiritual and everyday well-being. You can include disciplines of bedtimes and what is now often called 'sleep hygiene' in your Rule of Life. Many people have smart watches, apps and other gadgets that track sleep. These may be useful reminders, but they are not likely to be very reliable and it is important not to become obsessed about sleep. The more you think about something, the more you may be making things worse. If sleep is difficult, spiritual direction is an opportunity to put the issue in a broad context. The lack of sleep may be a result of many other things, and perhaps this is what you can explore. Perhaps in your life there is stress, exhaustion, worry and the mind does not easily let go. How might you help yourself? It is important to ask this, but beware of the ways in which we are invited to obsess about sleep by advertising. You do not have to look very far on the internet to find advice and lots of products, some very expensive, to help us sleep. It may be important to recognize the difference between symptoms and the causes of a lack of sleep. Be discerning. All the scented pillows in the world will not help if we are worried about something that is taking a lot of emotional and spiritual energy. Our way of life is often not sleep friendly and habits are hard to break. A review of our habits and some small changes is sometimes the place to start. The spiritual director will not offer facile solutions. You will keep experimenting and you will learn about shaping new patterns. Meanwhile, you are concerned with the spiritual implications and your spiritual resources. The spiritual director will be concerned with how your soul is faring, and will not take a problem-solving approach to these issues. Your soul needs sleep as much as your body, and soul work continues in those hours of rebalancing. There is a reason why we sometimes need to sleep on an issue, a decision or the sending of an email. While we rest, our soul is quietly offering wisdom from the depths. In those sleepless times, what is the conversation with God?

Preparing for spiritual direction

◇ Do I sleep well? How does sleep contribute to my spiritual well-being?

◇ When I do not sleep, do I have insight into the reasons why this is?

◇ What do I want to say about this in spiritual direction?

◇ Do I have a Rule of Life? Does it include attention to rhythms of rest and sleep?

◇ What is my prayer when I do not sleep?

Prayer

Thank you, God, for restorative sleep, renewing my body and my mind for life and work, decision-making and conversation.

In those hours when there is no sleep, draw me deeper into an understanding of myself, of you, and remind me of the preciousness of this gift for all people and all life.

Awake or asleep, may my soul find rest in you.

28

Doubt

When it comes to questions of doubt, spiritual directors will not be perturbed, in fact they will probably be quite pleased to hear about it. This is because expressions of doubt may well be a sign that there is healthy questioning going on, which will lead to a deeper understanding and integration of all that you believe and why, and how it is lived out.

Doubt may take many forms: it may be focused on what you believe, or whether you are doing the right thing, or whether you are following what God is calling you to be and do. You might be wondering what God is up to and why God appears not to do anything about suffering. Perhaps you wonder if there is any God at all. Perhaps you have been taught certain doctrines or ideas which you no longer find compelling and you want to dig deeper. If you are to continue on your path of faith, there are things you need to resolve.

Early in our lives, we pick up certain beliefs, values and ideas that we may accept because we have not yet learnt to critique our own experience. This comes much later, in the light of two particularly significant things we learn as we mature. Firstly, we come to understand that the authority figures in our lives may not always be right, because their information is based on what they learnt from a variety of sources. Secondly, we gather a lot more information and insight into other viewpoints and, while we might initially dismiss these, there may come a time when we wonder if alternatives are worth consideration. Alternative viewpoints may have been presented to us in a distorted or incomplete way, and we realize there is more to know. The only way to really understand another perspective is to go to the source, find out what it is really about from someone who knows for themselves.

Another thing happens to us as we grow up: we really want to understand the things that we are saying we believe. We may hear ourselves say something and wonder 'What do I really mean?' Or someone may ask us to explain something we believe and we realize that what we have to say is not very compelling. We do not need to fear that we are in danger of intellectualizing everything and taking trustful faith out of the equation. It is simply that a truth cannot be transformative unless we have internalized it, know its truth from the inside, all the way through, in understanding and experience. Sometimes you can hear a sermon or talk and you have the sense that the speaker is saying all the right things but their grasp is superficial, they have not been changed by the ideas they are sharing. When someone repeats what they read in a book, but they have not lived it out, we are unlikely to be convinced by the argument.

As you listen to others you will find yourself working out whether what you hear makes sense to you. Questioning does not mean doubting, it just means you are working out your own perspective. Mature spirituality is not satisfied with superficial or second-hand ideas. If something is true and life-giving, then it will be something that makes sense in our own lives. Making sense does not exclude faith, trust and hope in any way, it puts them into the whole perspective of our spirituality so that we can draw on trust and knowledge, reason and experience.

When we talk about doubt in a spiritual sense, we often mean that we doubt things that we think we are supposed to believe. A spiritual director will help you think through where that 'supposed to' might come from and whether it is a trustworthy voice.

'Doubt' is sometimes shorthand for doubting that God cares or exists at all. Our doubts may be helping us ask very pertinent questions, so we should listen to the so-called doubts in our soul. Maybe we are being invited to a bigger vision of

God, perhaps all we are doubting is the limited or narrow view that was formed in the light of the teaching we had or the community we were part of.

New information, new experience, new knowledge, all call us to constantly re-evaluate what we think we know. In some sense, our faith is always provisional, but not because it is uncertain or weak. A robust faith is strong enough to be interrogated, to develop, to be nuanced in the light of our growth. The humble soul is able to hold beliefs and perspectives confidently while also recognizing that it is always possible for new perspectives to emerge. In the future, I may learn something that casts today's beliefs in a completely different light and there is no need to be afraid of that. God is always bigger than our ideas, our fixed points. Tomorrow I may learn something that I simply cannot imagine or anticipate today.

Fundamentalism emerges from certainty which has no room for learning and is utterly closed to any new perspectives. Fundamentalism can draw neither on true reason nor generous compassion. Compassion is always a good reason to reassess what we believe. What are the fruits of our beliefs? If our frameworks of belief and our values lead us to lives without compassion then the most fundamental structures of the Kingdom of God are not in place.

A spiritual director will not try and keep you on the straight and narrow of faith as defined by anyone else, including them. They may encourage you to think more deeply theologically so that you can critique yourself, but they will not tell you how or what to believe. Perhaps some new avenues to explore will be offered but this is never more than an invitation. Living spirituality is a pilgrimage, a journey; there is no need to fear engaging with new ideas. You can always come back to your starting point if you find you are heading for a dead end. Think about the things that are points of principle for you, the 'tent pegs' that hold everything together. Tent pegs are a good metaphor for the things we believe because we can choose to have a lot of them, or it may be that our particular tent only needs two or three, or perhaps only 'Love'. Tent pegs are moveable, you can check they are in place and secure them, or you can relocate them. Spiritual direction will support this discernment. Spiritual resources, theologians, saints and poets may come to your aid. Whatever questions and agonies you have in your faith, probably someone else has wrestled with the same questions. You may find some insight in reading what others have said. You don't necessarily need to look for academic theology. Autobiographies can be informative, you can read about how writers have sought to bring their life experience together with their faith and how they have grown in understanding.

The soul is always on the move, always searching, curious and full of wondering. Listen for the questions, don't be afraid.

Preparing for spiritual direction

◇ What was I taught or came to believe early in my faith journey? Do any aspects of this seem less compelling now?
◇ What have I learnt that has made me nuance my beliefs?
◇ Have I had difficult experiences that have made me question who God is, how God works, or whether there is 'God' at all?
◇ What are the 'tent pegs' that hold my faith and sense of meaning in place? Do I need many or just a few? If I had only one thing to hold fast to, what would it be?

Prayer

Read the Psalms and look for a passage in which the psalmist is wrestling with God. What resonates with you? Stay with it over days, weeks or even months. Let it pray in you and for you.

You might like to prayerfully read the book of Job, though it may leave you with as many questions. Jonah is a much shorter account, read his story and see what you notice.

29

Nature

The theme of nature is included here because it is so often said that this is where God is encountered, whether climbing mountains or tending a garden. Nature has remarkable healing properties. By 'nature' I mean all that is growing and alive, as opposed to static, manufactured and in a process of disintegration. Nature decays; this is a natural process and not a bad thing, because organic decay means the recycling of elements. Disintegration may be a rather different process if it is not organic and essentially creative. Someone or something is needed to recreate, to reverse the process; it will not happen by itself. A tree that dies will recycle itself. A neglected building will either be overrun by nature, or someone might use the materials to make something new.

To be in nature, or in the presence of nature, is to be energized by the cycle of life. It reassures, challenges, renews and invites us. It is all around us hour by hour, day by day. Our lives are sustained by the seasons, though in the twenty-first century we must face the challenge of what is happening to the world we inhabit. The world is not our private property, although at times humankind has treated it as if we owned it and everything in it. We have even extended our sense of possession and domination to other people as well as land, sea, air, creatures and natural resources. The world is home for all, and while many living things take only what they need to live, we have gone way beyond that with our capacity to damage or even destroy it. This we may yet do, it is entirely possible. We have the advantages of self-awareness, science, memory and knowledge, whether we use them to engage intentionally and responsibly to protect the earth is the challenge of our age. One of the reasons nature is so powerful is that it takes no account at all of our self-importance. Birds, creatures, the elements are oblivious to our desires, our achievements, our failures and victories. Nature accepts us as we are and we can choose to be a guest or an intruder. When we come as a guest, remarkable moments of encounter may occur. Face to face with a creature as simple as a toad, or as nervous as a deer, can be a spiritual experience as engaging as any liturgy. Perhaps this is because we can only be in the present, there is nowhere else to go. The moment is fleeting and yet somehow eternal, you will remember every detail if you allow yourself to be fully present without reaching for the phone to grab a picture. The moment will be gone the second your attention moves away.

Nature requires attention from all our senses. The sight of the sea after a long walk towards the coast may evoke a physical sense of relief and joy, the sudden blast of cold wind on a coast path as you turn a corner out of shelter, these are felt with our senses and take root in our soul.

However, it is important not to romanticize nature. Beautiful views, lambs and woodpeckers may make us feel spiritually connected but what about the other side of life? You do not need to observe nature for long before you will see murder most foul. One day a stoat killed five baby rabbits outside our window while the parents looked on, paralysed with terror. A sparrowhawk plucked a blue tit from a bird feeder, and a magpie ripped into a harmless thrush collecting worms in the grass. Hardly material for a sentimental reflection on Spring. The Easter cards with their chicks and bunnies offer a more sanitized version of the season and don't draw attention to the fact that stoats and foxes, sparrowhawks and magpies also have young.

There is a danger too that exulting in nature can be the vocabulary of the privileged who have transport, access to gardens and can go on holiday. The many months of 'lockdown' during the height of the Covid pandemic highlighted this all too graphically. To work at home, or to have leisure, while being able to garden and take long walks in the countryside (even if alone) was a joy denied to many. Some barely saw daylight because of their work, others were severely restricted in their movements by responsibilities as carers or homeschoolers. We need to be very careful about our enthusiasm for the kind of spiritual experience less accessible to others. Nevertheless, we do not always have to head for the great outdoors. Even growing something on a windowsill invites wonder.

If we enjoy the hospitality of nature, we can both care for it and seek ways to ensure that no one is denied access because of their circumstances. In spiritual direction you can explore how gratitude can inform action.

Preparing for spiritual direction

◇ Have I had a nature moment that has stayed with me?
◇ Where do I go to experience green, growing, alive things?
◇ How can I invite nature into the places where I live and work?
◇ Do I look out for things that live and grow in unlikely places?
◇ How could I protect nature and help to ensure access for all?

Prayer

God of life, I celebrate beauty and wonder. Call me to love and protect your creation and challenge me when I fall into sentimentality or the shortsightedness of privilege.

30

Children

I write as a mother, and my own experience of childhood has informed the way I have related to my own children. My parents were children of their own time and influenced by the attitudes of previous generations as well as world events at the time. I have often had to remember that when tempted to critique the aspects of my childhood that I found difficult. To some extent, the way we relate to our own children is bound to be informed by our own experience, even when we are not aware of it. We may take the aspects that were positive, or which we simply took for granted, as a model. We may also react to what we experienced and resolve do the opposite.

Anyone who has children is likely to want to talk about it in spiritual direction sometimes. From the first moment you even think about the possibility of their arrival, children demand all you have within you and more. Your material and emotional resources and your spiritual life will sustain you, you will certainly need them. Babyhood and childhood require a lot of input from parents and caregivers. Later, there will be new relationships to learn. Children may find partners, and perhaps grandchildren arrive. When you meet your spiritual director for the first time, they may tell you a bit about their life, experience and circumstances. If there is common ground this may give you a sense that they will be able to empathize with you. However, although they may offer you some background, there will be a whole world that they keep to themselves. There will be joys and sorrows that you won't know anything about, because they will not want to impose either their joy or their grief on your story. Notice the quality of listening; whether their experience is similar or different, you will know by the way they listen to you if they have some insight and understanding.

I have listened to the challenges that come with having children. Children may arrive after years of waiting and longing, they be a surprise or even an interruption. They are a wonderful gift and a massive responsibility. We hope for joy in our children and often there is an abundance of that, it shines through the exhaustion. But children do not come with any guarantees. They may be lost, in many different ways, sometimes before they even arrive and sometimes along the way. The death of a child, at any age, or the rift in a relationship with a child you do not have contact with, is a grief beyond words.

What kinds of conversations about children might be had in spiritual direction? There are so many. Children make us happy, proud, nervous, anxious, sometime exasperated. They love school or they hate it, they find friends and they are hurt by the cruelty of other children. They learn fast and they struggle with learning. They adore us, fall out with us, don't get on with each other, move away, move back, experience relationships that last or don't last. They find jobs and move on from them, happily or otherwise. They make decisions we are not sure about. They do and say things we are amazed by and hugely proud of. We wonder how we can keep up, emotionally or spiritually.

What we bring to spiritual direction is not so much our children but our love, our self-doubt, our grief, our vulnerability and all our prayers that their lives will be all right. Sometimes we measure ourselves and our children against expectations that are completely unrealistic. The spiritual director may help us to hear ourselves and gently encourage us to judge ourselves less harshly.

We cannot be perfect. I sometimes say to my own children that I am setting an example of imperfection. If I was perfect (which is not likely to happen anytime soon) then they might feel they have to live up to it, so I am sparing them that.

When they were small, I was once asked by a reporter who was covering the first ordinations of women as priests in the Church of England if I hoped my daughters might 'follow me into the church'. It implied that I thought the best thing my children could do was imitate me, an idea that had no logic. I said I hoped they would find what they were meant to do. If you have more than one child you might wonder how they could be so different from their siblings, and maybe from you. When we think about it, this is not surprising at all, every individual is unique. In spiritual direction we can recognize where our own agendas might get in the way of being able to let go of our expectations and goals.

We carry our children in our souls always, it is where they belong.

Preparing for spiritual direction

◇ What do I need to explore around this theme? What does it mean for me? What experiences and questions am I living with?

◇ Where are my joys, griefs, vulnerabilities? Tell the story as it is.

◇ What is the conversation with God? What do I need?

Prayer

If you have the care of children, whether young or adult, name them in your prayers and ask for what you need to understand them and support them in their own lives.

31

Resentment

Resentment is like toothache, you cannot forget it, your attention is constantly drawn back to it. Every now and then you convince yourself that you are moving on and the issue is not a problem any more, then it jumps up and gives you a whole new wave of thoughts and feelings. Resentment disturbs, disrupts and distracts. You feel irritated with the cause and with yourself for letting things get to you. Your logic may tell you that your resentment is absolutely justified but it is still a horrible feeling. You are out of sorts with people and with yourself and, of course, God. All the while, you know that the person(s) you resent may have no idea what grief they have caused you and their lives are just carrying on quite happily. It does not seem fair at all and so we begin to resent not only what they did or did not do, but their unawareness of it as well.

When someone hurts or offends us, we sometimes feel that at least an apology would help. An apology is an acknowledgement of responsibility and an expression of regret at the hurt caused. The refusal to offer an apology, or the knowledge that the person does not think one is required, can seem to add insult to injury and is a cause of further resentment. This is why resentment is so toxic: it finds reasons to keep on multiplying itself.

A different kind of resentment is when someone is entirely innocent of wrongdoing but you resent their good fortune. Perhaps they were successful in some way you envied, or they seem to have more money, more friends, or just more fun. It may be that they display the kind of confidence you would like yourself and it is not really them you resent, but yourself.

Resentment self-replicates like a line of mirrors, the image just goes on and on and on. The only way out is to step right outside that whole perspective and reframe the whole way you are thinking about it.

It is hard to let go; no wonder people speak of 'nursing' or holding on to a grudge or a resentment. We grow rather fond of it perhaps, because it allows us to remind ourselves of our superiority, our moral standing, our innocence as victims of someone else. Because a part of us knows all this quite well, it is hard to bring to spiritual direction because we are ashamed. Resentment does not seem like a worthy emotion, it can be hard to admit that we feel it. If you belong to a community that celebrates kindness, you might worry that you will be judged as self-centred if you admit to struggling with feelings about other people.

The spiritual director may help by turning your attention elsewhere. Resentment is hard to address directly, but you can starve it of attention. Once your reasons for resentment are no longer centre stage, they may find a proper sense of perspective. Find things to celebrate, refuse to feed it and it will begin to lose its power.

Resentment is self-referential; not only do we resent the thing that was done or not done, said or not said, but we might also resent that someone else clearly does not love or care for us. When we let go of the need to be in the centre of someone else's adoration, we grow up. There may be reasons why we feel resentful that we can address, but our resentment is our own challenge. If someone tells me they resent me, I will tend to take the view that it is their problem and they need to get over it. If, on the other hand, they present me not with their feelings but with something I have said or done which affected them, I can consider whether I need to engage with that.

A spiritual director can point you in the right direction and recognize when you are too focused on yourself. They will not ridicule your genuine feelings, but they might gently wonder if your feelings are proportionate and encourage you to look at the situation from different angles.

Preparing for spiritual direction

◇ Where am I carrying resentment? Can I tell the story, unvarnished, without missing out the bits that don't paint me in a very favourable light?

◇ Can I listen to myself as I describe other people? What do I notice?

◇ Can I look at it from different angles?

◇ Is there something I can do, a symbolic act, a ritual or liturgy?

Prayer

Give me courage, O God, to recognize when my resentments are out of proportion. Help me to let go of the fear, the jealousy or anger that feeds the resentment. Help me to see my resentments for what they are and let them go.

32

Forgiveness

Forgiveness is a difficult and emotive subject, and an especially loaded word in the Christian tradition. To know that you are forgiven is to experience deep healing. Yet we often struggle to forgive both ourselves and others. Whether the emphasis is on giving it or receiving it, wanting it or not wanting it, forgiveness is complex. There are things that have wounded us and we wonder where forgiveness fits in. We wonder whether we can forgive or whether we even aspire to.

Forgiveness becomes even more complicated when we are thinking not so much of ourselves, but what has happened to our dear ones. Those close to us may have suffered and we are not sure if we can or want to forgive on behalf of loved ones. We may wonder if there are some things that cannot or should not be forgiven. We take comfort in God's forgiveness at times, yet we also want a God who delivers justice, and perhaps punishment too. We may wonder if there are some things that should never be forgiven.

It is important to think about what we understand by the concept of forgiveness. Forgiveness does not mean that something that is wrong no longer matters or that we have written it off. To forgive can mean that we continue to recognize a wrong yet choose not to live from a place of wishing ill on someone or hating them. We do not have to say that words or actions do not matter in order to choose to release our desire for punishment or revenge. This is very far from saying that there is no accountability or that there should not be consequences. Rather, we are choosing not to seek to administer that justice ourselves. At its simplest we might say it is a decision not to curse someone or put them in a box that we also fill with hate and malice. If I choose not to hold malice in my heart, I am making a choice about my own well-being and spiritual and mental health. I am not releasing someone else from their responsibilities or the consequences of their actions. To forgive someone does not mean that they should not go to prison or make restitution. We can seek to take a step back and choose not to hate and allow the processes of justice to take their course. Sometimes these let us down, deepening our distress. Spiritual direction offers a space to explore the conflicted feelings this will evoke.

Forgiving ourselves is another challenge. If we go through life with bitter regret or guilt, we will be unhappy and stunted in our spiritual growth. We sometimes feel we do not deserve forgiveness, but forgiveness is never a matter of deserving. It is free, generous and liberating because God is a God of healing and possibility.

Forgiveness doesn't make much sense outside of some kind of spiritual framework. If there was no spiritual context, we would have no reason not to feel what we feel and think what we think and direct those thoughts and feelings where we wished. For Christians the notion of forgiveness is rooted in God's grace. The Christian tradition draws on an older story and is rooted in that of the Jewish people whose history is recounted in the Hebrew Bible. In both traditions, God is known as full of mercy and grace. Sometimes people say that the Old Testament portrays a God who is vengeful and angry, in contrast with the message of the New Testament where Jesus is the representative of a loving and compassionate God. These ideas misrepresent the Hebrew Bible and the Jewish tradition as well as creating a false contrast with Christian teaching, misrepresenting the message of Jesus. Certainly the Hebrew Bible contains some violent narratives, but a God of mercy, compassion and grace is very much present and throughout Scripture we are constantly called back to reconciliation with God and with the world. Again and again the Hebrew Bible underlines grace and mercy, and reminds us that God is tender and compassionate. It may not be easy to reconcile this with the more challenging texts, but we cannot say that the God of the Old Testament is simply a God of judgement.

Anger and a desire for revenge, even in circumstances where there has been terrible injustice, always tend to draw us away from God in the end. We have to find ways to deal with it rather than prolong it. But to simply talk about forgiveness as if this were an obvious and simple thing do does not really work. We cannot make ourselves generate a sense of forgiveness. Forgiveness is not a feeling any more than love or kindness are feelings. It is hard, slow work, and the spiritual director will not hurry you along. You decide each next step and name how you feel and what you carry. The spiritual director may draw you back to your image of God and your relationship with God. We can only view others from the place we are with God ourselves. We cannot be kind without having known kindness, or be generous without having known generosity. If we cannot extend forgiveness, there may be more for us to receive first.

A spiritual director will not expect you to ignore, deny or minimize wrongdoing. The conversation is about your internal disposition, and finding a more peaceful place does not mean saying that wrong does not matter. This is what often gets in the way as we try to process the things we find hard to forgive. You may go round in circles, you may feel trapped in difficult feelings, but keep going, there is a more life-giving place and the spiritual director will be quietly accompanying you while you travel.

Preparing for spiritual direction

◇ Where have I received forgiveness in my own life? What have I learnt from this?

◇ Have I a sense of being able to forgive others for past events? What was important for me in these situations? What did I learn about myself, about God, about life?

LISTENING TO YOUR SOUL

◇ Are there things I struggle to let go of? What does the idea of forgiveness mean to me? Where would I like to get to on this journey of releasing wounds and hurts?

◇ What do I need to forgive myself for?

Prayer

God of unending mercy and grace, I rest in you. Widen my perspectives, deepen my generosity, teach me to relinquish hatred and violence in my soul.

33

Employment

Employment is not the same as 'work'. You may work very hard but not be employed and those who are not in paid employment can feel undervalued and unrecognized. There may be long hours given to caring for others or undertaking work they believe in but which is not remunerated.

For those who have a 'job' that requires them to undertake certain functions and be accountable to other people or an organization, there will always be spiritual challenges. The work may suit you very well, or it may be not at all what you would choose to do. It is not always easy to change your paid work, there are so many factors that have led us to do the work we have taken on. Stories of people who have taken a risk and thrown off the expectations and security of their working lives can be inspiring but don't necessarily offer a realistic example to follow. You may have responsibilities to members of your family, and this makes it hard to simply please yourself and head off round the world or fulfil your dream of living on a boat or a smallholding.

For the moment, if you have a job to do it is likely that you will talk about it in spiritual direction. Whether your work is part-time or all-consuming, it will demand mental and emotional energy and spiritual resources. Perhaps the work is vocational in some way, perhaps it does not seem so. When your job does not seem like a vocation in terms of the tasks and responsibilities involved, you can feel trapped and unmotivated. However, you need not despair of living vocationally. It is always possible to be yourself, the person God has called you to be, in your work context. Perhaps you can consider how to live in a vocational way in the context of a job that does not in itself feel like a 'calling'. Who are you called to be? Can you live out this call in the context of your work?

How did you come to be in the particular work you do now? The path may be the outworking of many factors, including possibility, location, other people, finance. You may have changed roles within the same organization and that is not always an improvement.

In spiritual direction you can reflect on how God fits into all this, and what it means to respond to God now in these circumstances. We may be grateful, frustrated, bored, but whatever we are experiencing, our work will be a part of our spiritual life too.

Relationships at work can be a huge challenge and you can bring the workplace politics and processes to spiritual direction. This is your daily reality, the context of your discipleship and ministry. Talk about what it is like, with all the aspects that frustrate you or try your patience.

You may want to think about your theology of guidance as well as your understanding of work. Does God have a purpose in leading you to, or leaving you in, this place? You need not assume that your situation is necessarily 'God's will'. Explore your understanding in spiritual direction.

We cannot always change where we are, but we may be able to think about 'how' we are where we are. A spiritual director will listen as you explore this and find ways to 'be'. How might your soul be present to inform and enliven your work, its purpose, the relationships around it and its place in your life?

Preparing for spiritual direction

◇ What is it like to be in my job? How do I understand God's guidance and purpose in relation to how I came to be here?

◇ Who am I called to be? What qualities and gifts can I bring to my work context and the people around me?

◊ What do I need from God in order to flourish and thrive in my work circumstances?

Prayer

Every day, may I enter into my work with compassion and hope.
What gifts, O God, can I carry into my workplace?
What light and peace might I hold in this place, here and now?

34

Choices

We make countless choices every day, from what to have for breakfast to what to put in a tricky email. Some are not given a thought, others we agonize over. Some are costly, some are generous, some are scarcely choices at all because they are compulsive, habitual or addictive. We have both more and less choice than we imagine, acknowledge or realize sometimes. Personality, experience and complex working of the brain all play a part. Social pressures, culture, religious beliefs, family, advertising, all have an influence and may mean that we are not always as free in our decisions as we would like, or that we knowingly compromise in our choices because of circumstances or people that will be affected.

When we are thinking about choices that are prayerfully made in the light of our spiritual reference points, we might use the word 'discernment'. Discernment means more than simply choosing this or that. It involves weighing options and possibilities and seeking to take the path that is truly wise and life-giving. We might also ask which path brings glory to God, or reflects the Kingdom of God, or best embodies compassion.

The Ignatian tradition uses the language of discernment and if you go on an Ignatian-style retreat you will probably meet with a spiritual director each day. Depending on the nature and purpose of your retreat, you might find the conversation turning to discernment. This may mean reflection on the ways in which you experience coming closer to God, which is sometimes referred to as consolation. At other times you may experience a sense of being drawn away from God. This is sometimes called desolation, though it does not necessarily mean that we feel miserable, just that we are not being drawn closer to God. Ignatian spirituality and spiritual direction is not the focus of this book, but it is something to be aware of, especially if someone asks you if that is the kind of spiritual direction you are looking for. Many spiritual directors are trained in the Ignatian tradition, but they will not necessarily use the particular tools of this approach in an explicit way all the time. A spiritual director will tell you if they have been trained in this way and explain how it informs their practice of spiritual direction.

Discernment is the fruit of wisdom. We do not always know what the 'right' thing to do is, and we may not be sure if the 'right' thing is something we desire, or whether the right thing is going to be something difficult and costly. Once again we have to think about what kind of God we know and relate to. Some people imagine that God takes some kind of pleasure in asking us to do difficult things. If we believe that, even unconsciously, we may assume that there will be a good chance that God wants us to do the more unpleasant thing. This is distorted thinking, but if it is how you feel, talk about it in spiritual direction and acknowledge your fears. You may come to smile at yourself when you remember the generosity of God.

In spiritual direction you can explore what is really important to you and why, and how much effort or compromise you might be willing or able to make. It is hard work to find more freedom in our habits, and the reasons for motivation can be complex. Your spiritual director will be listening for what is realistic and what may be fanciful. Where are you over- or under-estimating your options and your capacities?

If something is making you hesitate about a big change, explore where that hesitation lies. Listen to the deepest invitation of your soul. What might be the steps to different choices?

Preparing for spiritual direction

◇ What choices am I facing at the moment? What is important to me?
◇ What influences the choices I make every day? Do I sense a need to make different choices?
◇ What choices have I made in the past and what did I learn from that experience?
◇ Are there areas of life where I do not feel free, where I make choices that are driven by habits, compulsion or addiction?

Prayer

Today, I choose life. Show me the path of life, the path of freedom and generosity. I choose to let go of small agendas, petty obsessions, and embrace beauty, hope, imagination.

35

Regret

Regret is something familiar to everyone. It ranges from low-level irritation at a minor mistake to a gut-wrenching agony because of a misjudgement or momentary foolishness, oversight or accident. No one can turn the clock back, but in our distress we long to return to the moment before we committed to a course of action. Our minds drag us back in a futile attempt to wipe the video and re-record, something we are very used to doing in other parts of life where we have control.

We have no control over the passing of time and things that have already happened. Regret is what we feel when we are thinking about actions, words and choices that we have made, but the tragedy is that they were not inevitable. Regret is so painful precisely because of the element of 'if only'. We imagine the scenarios in which we did, or did not do, the things we failed to do or commit to. Rumination is pointless, the moment has passed and we have to live with the consequences for ourselves and for others.

We may be able to turn things around to some extent in due course but in the immediate moment of regret, our minds are not future focused, not yet imagining possibility. Even when we do glimpse an alternative route, it may feel very much like second best. However, we cannot dwell on 'if only'. 'If only' is a fantasy that merely deepens our distress. There is no 'if only', but it takes time to accept this and move on.

Regret in relation to life-changing events may be more traumatic than the focus of a spiritual direction conversation can hold. If counselling or therapy is helpful, this will reframe things, perhaps over a long period, and during this time spiritual direction may continue as a prayerful, supportive context in which to focus on the conversation with God. In spiritual direction, much of the time, we may be bringing things that seem much more significant to us than they do to other people. Regret may lead us to think that the world is judging us, holding us in contempt and despising us, but it is possible that the only person with these judgements is us. We usually judge ourselves far more harshly than other people do. In prayer, listening and receiving, we may gradually become more able to hear God's tender voice telling us that all is well, that we are loved.

Regret will pass in its own time, but in its first stages it can be almost unbearably sharp. We feel it in our whole body. We cannot avoid this pain, but it is worth remembering that what seems so humiliating today will fade tomorrow, and we will have found a way to hold our experiences and feelings. Life is constantly being renegotiated and recalibrated and our perspectives will change. As a new course is charted, we will judge ourselves less harshly and come to see that what seemed disastrous at the time is not necessarily so. Of course, if we have caused real harm or suffering to others by our actions then that is a different, more complex conversation which might involve mediation or facilitation as well as therapeutic support.

One way of looking at our regrets is to consider how much we judge others for the things they regret. Probably not as much as we imagine we are judged. Consider how you would look at your actions and words if it was someone dear to you that had done these things. Would you be generous, affirming and supportive in your approach?

Preparing for spiritual direction

◇ What do I regret most keenly?
◇ How do I experience regret in my body?
◇ Do I imagine a different past and a different future? Can I move on from 'if only'?

◇ Are there regrets in my life which are unresolved because of the way other people are affected? What do I want to say about this in spiritual direction and are there things I need to do?

◇ Are there long-standing regrets I might take to the grave? Is it too late? Might I seek some help?

Prayer

I centre my attention in this present moment.
I give thanks for all that is.
I hold before God the things I regret.
I ask for peace and wisdom. Give me courage to take responsibility but not to be trapped or condemned by self-referential focus.
Recognizing the sharp sting of regret, I commit to supporting others who punish themselves needlessly.

36

Ageing

There is a lot of popular wisdom around getting older. People merrily say that 'you're as young as you feel' or 'age is only a number'. There may be some truth in these attitudes, but in the end ageing is not negotiable and we do not have control over all its effects. We express surprise when we discover people are older than we guessed they might be. If we hear they are older than we assumed we react to that in a variety of ways. Perhaps they are to be commended for keeping up appearances. Perhaps we feel sorry because they might be nearer to death than we thought. We need to be alert to the possibility of ageism, with its potential for discrimination and prejudice. This is more of an issue in some cultures than others. In some communities, ageing people are valued, whereas in others they are pitied, despised or even feared because they remind us of what our own future may hold.

There is plenty of advice and encouragement available to keep going, keep active, stay positive, look after ourselves. Some of this is good, health-conscious information, and quite a lot is advertisement-driven. There are numerous products and facilities that appeal to our fear of being unfit or immobile. Some people are able to ignore their health, because they see no reason to be concerned. This may or may not be a wise strategy, at worst it is a 'head in the sand' approach one might later regret. Others worry about the numerous possibilities for deterioration of mind or body, and these concerns may be well-founded or not, depending on the information available. Our approach to our own health is very personal. Some people are deeply private, even seeming secretive, while others broadcast to the world everything that happens in their bodies and every piece of medical information they have been given.

No one is alive who was on the earth two hundred years ago. We can hold off death for only so long. Ageing brings much to celebrate, but it will not let us forget that we only have so long. For some, there is no tragedy in that, few people really want to live for ever and the physical and mental aspects of becoming older are not always easy to navigate.

Life is unpredictable, and when we know we are ageing we may be thankful to have got to the point where ageing is a 'thing'. Perhaps the death of parents brings home our mortality as much as anything. As long as parents are alive, we are not on the last bus and we can pretend that journey is a long way off. When parents have gone, we are the next generation and with each year more contemporaries and family members will be lost from our lives.

What is the conversation for spiritual direction? It will depend on what we are thinking and feeling. Ageing can be bittersweet. As we get older, we are free of the concerns that bothered us in childhood, teens or young adulthood. The battles we had, the struggles and anxieties, are not ones we have to inhabit or repeat. Perhaps the prospect of retirement has kept us positive through some challenging times and it finally arrives with the promise of travel, leisure or whatever we have not been able to enjoy until that time arrived. But for some there is no golden promise of dreams fulfilled, but rather the prospect of continued struggles.

Later years can allow us to be more self-sufficient and secure, perhaps reaping the harvest of hard work, savings, establishing a home and family. These things may then begin to slip away, sooner than we thought, to be lost as we become frail and dependent. Many of us fear incapacity of mind or body and we do what we can to avoid it, but the reality is that we have limited control over how we age. Even the healthiest regimes do not come with guarantees and at some point it is spiritual fitness that will be our greatest resource. Like any other fitness, spiritual health does not arrive automatically. We practise minor adjustments, give small things up and release our grip on the relatively unimportant things. Perhaps, after a lifetime of learning to know the true value of all things, ageing will not come with fear and resistance but with thankfulness and hope. Many spiritual directors are ageing people who bring a lifetime of experience and, as they listen to you, are negotiating their own ageing.

Preparing for spiritual direction

◇ What has informed my attitude to ageing? What assumptions have I encountered in my family or my community? What is healthy and not so healthy about those perspectives?
◇ Do I think about ageing and death? What questions do I avoid?
◇ What thoughts, prayers, hopes bring me peace?

Prayer

I place before you my fears, questions, anxieties. Help me neither to run from them nor be captured by them.
Thank you for the years I have had and for those to come. Help me to celebrate what can be celebrated and to relinquish what I cannot hold on to.

37

Time

In order to make space to speak with a spiritual director, you will need to give enough time to travel to the conversation, talk awhile and travel back. It would be a good idea if you also had time to prepare a little beforehand and reflect afterwards. It is not easy to have a spiritual direction conversation right in the middle of a busy working day. Any spiritual practice, including spiritual direction, requires an awareness of how you use time in your life. Many of us feel that we have never have enough, perhaps for others there seems to be too much.

A common theme in spiritual direction is how to live in the midst of the responsibilities we carry in our lives with their demands and relationships. Finding time to relax is a challenge for many, and there is also the desire to find time for prayer, reading, stillness and soul nourishment through creativity, being outdoors or spending time with others.

There are many tools for organizing our lives, whether on paper or electronic. You may have tried a number of them and found them more or less helpful. But there is no magic solution, and in the end we have to do the best we can. Your spiritual director will help you to think about what the real issues might be. You might need to take some practical steps to organize your time, but there may also be questions of priorities and boundaries. Learning to make choices, to be free in our yes and no, takes a lifetime of practice. When we take control of our time there is always some kind of compromise, and other people's priorities and values may not dovetail with ours. Learn to be secure and neither overly boundaried nor undiscerning in your giving of time. It is simply not possible to do and achieve all the things we might want to. Somewhere along the line we have to be reconciled to the reality of that and consider what our principles are. There are some daily habits that are foundational to you. There may be obligations, work, commitments and things that we simply enjoy. Think about what is really important and why. We cannot do everything, and it is inevitable that some things have to be relinquished.

The spiritual direction conversation will not solve all your time management problems, but you might find some new perspectives. Our use of time can evoke anxiety, guilt, even despair. Underneath these feelings there may be questions about our worth, our security, our purpose. Until we have considered these, we are unlikely to resolve our ongoing struggle with the to-do list.

As well as hourly and daily time, our lives have seasons. This is another theme for spiritual direction. What does your soul tell you about the season you are in? There are seasons for productivity and for reflection, for study and for healing and renewal. It is wise to pay attention to the seasons of the soul. Listen to your longings and desires, they will tell you what you need.

Preparing for spiritual direction

◇ What thoughts and emotions are associated with 'time' for me?
◇ Am I at peace with time or always fighting it?
◇ What beliefs about myself or about God lie underneath my relationship with time?
◇ Do I feel I have enough time? Why or why not? What for?
◇ Can I learn to rest in the fullness of now?

Prayer

God, you are beyond time and yet you act in it and
through it.
Give me wisdom to use the time you have given me.
May I be generous yet bounded, free yet measured,
always present, always open to the unexpected invitation
of this moment.

38

News

At any given time, the 'News' is likely to be disturbing, challenging and distressing as well as interesting and informative. We cannot run from world events or pretend they are nothing to do with us. Some things touch us more than others, but you may notice that the news stories you find most upsetting are the ones that invite you to recognize that they could so easily be your story. A news item can take people or communities previously unrecognized or unremarkable suddenly into the spotlight. A sensitive person will realize that 'this could so easily be me'. This could be my life, my story. We are reminded of the unpredictability of life and the apparent randomness of tragic events.

How do we engage with the constant flow of news which reaches us through screens of various kinds, through reports and images and discussion? Some people become overwhelmed and distressed to the point of not being able to function. Others turn away and cannot engage, choosing to stop listening because it is all too much.

What place does spiritual direction have? Spirituality can never simply be about our personal or private concerns. Spirituality is connection. Prayer is connection. We cannot simply park what happens far from where we live.

Connection is felt in our bodies. We are embodied souls and so when we hear distressing news we may know shock, horror and grief in our bodies as well as our minds. This is hard to bear, but it is part of our connectedness and actually therefore is prayer. The distress we feel when we hear of violence and tragedy is the response of our bodies and souls saying 'This matters, we are part of it.' We can acknowledge this physical and mental pain as prayer, the cry of our souls and bodies. It happens because we are connected.

Prayer may include petitions, intercessions, requests. If these are hard to frame because it feels like telling God what to do, or because we do not believe in the kind of God who needs lists or who starts and stops wars, then take courage and simply be connected.

We should not underestimate the power of connection. Silence, vigils, liturgies, rituals and protests connect us. To acknowledge connection is to pray.

Preparing for spiritual direction

◇ How am I affected by news?
◇ How do I respond to what is difficult and distressing? Do I take the option of denial or pray from a distance and hope that God will do something?
◇ How do I pray? What action could I take?

Prayer

God, take my response, in my mind, my body and soul,
as prayer.

Sit in silence and allow the connection with those who are suffering to become prayer.

Frequently asked questions

What is the difference between spiritual direction and spiritual accompaniment?

Generally speaking, this is a matter of emphasis and preference. For all practical purposes, they are the same thing. Training courses and networks may use the language of direction or accompaniment, but they refer to the same ministry. Some people prefer the word 'accompanier' because it emphasizes the lack of hierarchy in the relationship. Others would rather keep the traditional word 'director', while underlining the fact that the space is one to find direction together, in the context of listening to God who is the true director.

What is a soul friend?

The concept of soul friend has a long history and can be used to speak about a spiritual direction relationship. More usually, a soul friendship is a long-standing, possibly mutual, deep connection. A soul friend would probably not be someone you had a 'professional' relationship with, the relationship might be more like your relationships with friends or family members or people in your church, though with particular depth and honesty on both sides. A soul friend is someone you are able to share deeply with and who knows you through and through. They have your best interests at heart and are faithful to you, being able to say hard things when necessary.

Do you have to have religious faith to have a spiritual accompanier?

Anyone who desires to explore the spiritual dimension of life may be interested in finding a spiritual accompanier. What is important is that you find someone who is open to your perspectives and has some understanding of the kind of conversation you are looking for. Some spiritual accompaniers feel called to work within their own religious tradition, while others are happy to journey with anyone on a spiritual path, however that is described. When you contact a potential accompanier, tell them what you are looking for in the conversation and they will tell you if they might be the right person. There are lots of spiritual directors and accompaniers who are completely open about where you are coming from and will let you set the agenda.

How do I find a spiritual director / spiritual accompanier?

You may live in the area covered by an Anglican diocese or another church denomination or network. Anglican dioceses are easy to find on the internet and if you search for spiritual direction, spiritual accompaniment or spirituality, you may be able to find someone who can point you in the right direction. Many dioceses have an adviser for spirituality. Anglican networks are usually ecumenical and their lists include people of many traditions. They can also help you find an accompanier even if you do not attend an Anglican church. At the end of the book you can find some links to other networks who may be able to help.

What will a spiritual director ask me?

When you first make contact, the spiritual director will probably ask you what you are looking for and suggest an initial meeting. They might invite you to tell them a bit about yourself, but they will not ask you lots of questions, you can disclose as much or as little as you want to and take it from there. This first meeting is usually just to explore and see if you make a connection. There is no obligation on either side to take the conversation forward so do not be concerned if you do not feel the person is right for you.

Does it matter if I don't really know what I believe?

The whole point of spiritual direction is for you to have a space to explore your beliefs, perspectives and spiritual practices. If you had it all sorted out there might not be a lot to talk about, so do not worry if you feel confused, uncertain or a bit lost. The spiritual director will not push you to become clearer about your beliefs, you can work things out in your own time.

Do I have to pay for spiritual accompaniment?

Many spiritual directors ask for a fee or some kind of donation, others do not. A competent director will tell you at the outset what they normally expect so you are not embarrassed or nervous about asking. Some spiritual directors see this as a voluntary ministry, their way of serving others, and they may be able to do so because they are retired or supported in other ways. There are practitioners who offer spiritual direction alongside counselling, coaching or mentoring and therefore the arrangements are in line with their professional practice for these roles. Some spiritual directors have a fixed charge, others ask that you make a donation, as much as your wish or can afford. The spiritual director may need some contributions in order to be able to do this work, but if not, then they may ask that you make a contribution to a charity or religious order. Sometimes, the agreement is that you give what you might earn in an hour yourself or they may have a sliding scale to account for different circumstances. Some spiritual directors keep space to be able to give their time to one or two people who would not have the resources to pay anything. The subject of payment is a sensitive one both for directors and those coming for direction. Many people prefer a straightforward relationship and want to pay because it takes a sense of indebtedness out of the relationship. For some, paying the spiritual director is as natural as paying a hairdresser, but not everyone sees it this way. The important thing is that you are comfortable with the arrangement you have with your accompanier.

How do I know I can trust the spiritual director?

There are some key questions to ask. It is wise to establish what training they have had and where they are currently accountable. A spiritual director should have their own director and receive supervision. Supervision does not mean that the director talks about you to someone else, it is where they take their own inner work which arises from their ministry. The spiritual director will explain this to you, and they will tell you what limits might apply to the confidential nature of the relationship. You should expect complete confidentiality, unless you or someone else is at risk. The director should belong to a network that offers ongoing training and that may hold the responsibility for safeguarding training. Some networks will only list spiritual directors who have undergone safeguarding training, and this is a constantly-changing area with regard to requirements. Many church denominations offer training that covers areas relating to ministerial good practice, responding to domestic abuse and spiritual abuse. As spiritual direction is not a validated or accredited role, anyone can call themselves a spiritual director. This means that in theory they could function in an isolated way, so ask what networks the director belongs to and who they are accountable to. You should know who you would contact if anything in your conversation concerned you or made you feel uncomfortable or unsafe. Spiritual directors should be covered by insurance arrangements, either by the networks they belong to, or because they have taken out private insurance. This insurance means that they will have resources if someone holds them accountable for an accident on their premises, or an accusation of malpractice. A competent director will explain all the aspects of the relationship that you might be concerned about and sometimes they will give you a written agreement or contract. If they do not do this, then you can ask for something in writing that makes everything clear. The Retreat Association (details at the end of the book) has some guidelines on looking for a spiritual director which are clear and helpful. Many spiritual directors follow the guidelines for good practice which the Retreat Association offers and they may tell you this.

What do I do if a spiritual director says or does something I am not happy about?

It is important to trust your instincts. Depending on the circumstances, you might be able to discuss it with them. If that is not appropriate you can certainly withdraw from any further conversation. If it is a serious matter, in relation to the safety and integrity of the conversation, you may need to talk to someone else. This is why it is good at the outset to know where a spiritual director is accountable. This would be a rare scenario, but it could happen, so if in doubt, don't go back to that person and make sure you talk to someone. If you have been put in touch through a network, contact the person who is responsible for that network.

Is spiritual direction the same as going to confession?

If part of your spiritual practice is to make your confession to a priest from time to time, you might wonder if this is what happens in spiritual direction. They are not at all the same thing, although some spiritual directors do offer sacramental confession either as part of the meeting or at another time by arrangement. 'Confession' refers to a range of prayers which may be quite formal and liturgical, or may take a more informal, but nevertheless, structured and intentional approach. You may be familiar with this way of prayer, and it may be important to you. You can ask the director if this is something they offer.

Can I see a spiritual director just once or it is a regular thing?

Spiritual direction is most usually a relationship that develops over time, and you get to know each other quite well. However, you may want a particular conversation at a particular time, seek someone out, and the conversation may cover the ground you need it to and there is no need to continue. You might meet just once, or agree to meet for a limited period in order to focus on a particular agenda. One common practice is to meet for six sessions and then review.

How often should I see a spiritual director?

Spiritual direction is a conversation that allows both continuity and distance. If you meet very often there may be a running narrative and perhaps a sense of dependency which is not appropriate for spiritual direction. Some therapeutic conversations involve meeting very regularly, but they have a different purpose and dynamic. Spiritual direction is like a snapshot; you can talk about how things are, with or without reference to previous conversations. If you meet about every six to eight weeks you will find that there is enough recollection to support a developing relationship, but also the recognition that you may now be in a very different place. The director will not assume that life is as it was a few weeks ago and will come to the conversation without being prejudiced by previous events. There are exceptions to this general pattern. At times of crisis, you might want to be in touch more frequently. At other times, you might need a break in order to make space for major life events or to engage with a period of coaching or counselling.

Can I have more than one spiritual director?

It is really not a good idea to try and have more than one person in this role. You can of course share your heart and soul with anyone you trust and talk with, but spiritual direction is a very intentional conversation and best kept distinct and discrete. You might briefly converse with another director on a retreat, but that will have a short-term focus. Too many conversations will cause confusion. There may be many people you share with, or have spiritual conversation with, but having lots of spiritual directors is not advisable.

Do I need to know about the Bible or other spiritual writings?

No, you can refer to whatever sources are important to you, or none at all. You might want to talk about scriptures that have spoken to you, or even poetry, novels or art. But you are not expected to know about anything. There are no prerequisites for spiritual exploration, learn as you go.

Where do you meet a spiritual director to talk?

Usually you will travel to the spiritual director's home or another place where they meet people. Sometimes they may suggest that you meet in a public place such as a coffee shop. This can feel safe and reassuring, especially if you do not know each other, but it is usually too noisy for reflective conversation. Sometimes a spiritual director may come to you, especially if you are not mobile, and you can ask if they are willing and able. This does change the dynamic of the relationship and there are advantages, spiritually and emotionally, in going out and away from your environment, so this is usually the preferred option.

Can I talk about my own poetry or artwork?

Yes, you can talk about whatever you like and, if you are creative, your work may be an excellent way to reflect on things that are hard to express. A spiritual director will be interested in whatever you have written or made, they will listen to what it means to you without interpreting it or judging it.

How do spiritual directors come to be doing this work?

Usually they will have appreciated the direction or accompaniment they have received for themselves and over time have increasingly felt drawn towards listening to others. Often it starts to happen very naturally and gradually. Spiritual direction is not a career choice and not something a person sets out to do to please themselves in some way, it simply evolves. Most often, a person finds that people are talking with them naturally. Then they may feel they need to seek out some training to support their practice and learn more.

Is spiritual direction really a form of counselling but in a religious way?

Spiritual direction is distinct from counselling in many ways, though there will be points of contact or overlap. The key focus in spiritual direction is always how you are experiencing and responding to the presence and movement of the divine in your life. Spiritual direction is not a 'therapy' and the accompanier does not diagnose your state or determine what you need to do. Their role is to help you listen to your own soul and to God and to discern your own path. It is possibly to receive spiritual direction and counselling or therapy at the same time, though you should tell your spiritual accompanier that you are engaged in these conversations.

Do spiritual directors know about mental health issues?

Training in spiritual direction does not include specialist knowledge of mental health or other areas of psychology. Some spiritual directors may happen to have training in this area because of other experience or roles, but spiritual direction is not an appropriate context in which to diagnose or address mental health issues. Spiritual direction may be of great support during times of distress and illness, but it is not an alternative to trained therapeutic intervention. Even when a spiritual director has knowledge or expertise in this area, they will keep the conversation on the spiritual direction agenda, and if you need support with your mental health they will suggest that you address this in a different context. It is not good practice to mix different kinds of conversations as they have different boundaries and dynamics.

Can I ask my own vicar or pastor (or other spiritual leader or teacher) for spiritual direction?

Vicars, pastors, teachers and others in a spiritual community may well offer spiritual support and pastoral care and this is a normal part of church life. However, spiritual direction requires a little more distance to be really fruitful, and you will find that you are able to be more honest and open away from your church context, where there will be many overlapping relationships. Your minister, pastor or vicar will be concerned for you and may be a good listener. They do, however, have a particular role to fulfil and you will probably meet in other contexts, which is not always helpful to the spiritual direction relationship. One advantage of finding spiritual direction away from your church community is that you can be completely honest because a spiritual director is not invested in your spiritual life in any way, whereas a pastor or minister is likely to have at least some opinion about your spiritual welfare. Spiritual direction sometimes involves re-evaluating faith and as part of this journey you might want to change the way you engage with your church, or even leave it. You need to be able to speak freely about these things.

Can spiritual direction happen on Zoom or FaceTime or on the phone?

Spiritual direction can happen in any place and with whatever means are available and accessible.

Zoom or other video platforms are now commonplace and work well. They have the advantage of being able to meet across long distances. Something is inevitably lost when meeting in this way, but perhaps other things are gained. It is best to see video as one way to meet which is neither better nor worse than physically being in the same location, it is simply another possibility. Letter writing used to be the way to communicate but this is uncommon now. Email may be useful, but it is not really the equivalent of a carefully-composed handwritten letter, or even a typed one. Every form of communication has advantages and drawbacks. The phone is good for some who do not like Skype or Zoom. Cues, silences, pauses and non-verbal communication work differently in different contexts. The important thing is to discover what works for you and be aware of the ways in which you might need to compensate for communication 'blind spots'. The important thing is to understand the dynamics and features of the particular mechanism you have chosen and use it as effectively as you can.

Useful links

The Retreat Association
Promotes retreats, places for retreat and has some information and guidance about spiritual direction.
www.retreats.org

Sarum College, Salisbury
Provides a wide range of courses on many aspects of spirituality and a network of spiritual directors.
www.sarum.ac.uk

London Centre for Spiritual Direction
Provides courses, training and resources and a network of spiritual directors.
www.lcsd.org

The Association for Pastoral Supervision and Education (APSE)
Primarily a network for those supervising pastoral ministers, counsellors, chaplains and spiritual directors, but a number of people on the online directory do offer spiritual direction.
www.pastoralsupervision.org.uk

St Beunos
Offers retreats with spiritual direction in the Ignatian tradition.
www.beunos.com

Spiritual Direction UK forum
A recently-formed network for spiritual directors and to support the ministry of spiritual direction.
www.sdforum.uk

Further Reading

Sometimes people ask a spiritual director to recommend some reading. This is quite a tricky request for at least two reasons. First, there are so many possibilities it is hard for a spiritual accompanier to suggest just the right thing. Second, the spiritual director may have read some wonderful books and found them enormously helpful, but that does not mean they are right for anyone else. It is easy as a spiritual director to mislead someone by enthusing about what we have found helpful. It is also true that the most life-changing books I have read were discovered almost by accident – a coming together of time and place and perhaps something I never would have looked for. Sometimes, a book that at any other time might have meant nothing is so pertinent it takes your breath away. Here are a few suggestions of books that may take you down a gentle path of discovery. These books make connections between ordinary life and a spiritual perspective. They are engaging, down to earth and accessible, yet may also offer a note of challenge. Some include practical exercises or questions to reflect upon. Some authors have written other books and if you like their approach you can explore their writing further. This list could be very long, but here is a selection of recommended books.

Marcus Borg, *The Heart of Christianity*, HarperCollins San Francisco, 2003.
Barbara Brown Taylor, *An Altar in the World*, Canterbury Press, 2009.
Barbara Brown Taylor, *Learning to Walk in the Dark*, Canterbury Press, 2014.

Diana Butler Bass, *Grounded*, HarperOne, 2017.
Gerard W. Hughes, *God, Where are You?*, Darton, Longman and Todd, 1997.
Beverly Lanzetta, *Radical Wisdom*, Fortress, 2005.
Anthony de Mello, *Awareness*, Fount, 1997.
Thomas Moore, *Care of the Soul*, Piatkus, 1992.
Julia Mourant, *Listening to Your Life*, Canterbury Press, 2016.
J. Philip Newell, *Echo of the Soul*, Canterbury Press, 2002.
John O'Donohue, *Anam Cara*, Bantam, 1997.
Richard Rohr, *Everything Belongs*, Crossroad, 2003.
Richard Rohr, *Immortal Diamond*, Jossey Bass, 2013.